MEMORIES II-The Marines, The South and Family.

DEDICATION:

TO MY LATE WIFE ROBERTA, MY THREE SONS, MY GRANDCHILDREN, MY MOM AND DAD, MY GRANNY, THE MILITARY, LAW ENFORCEMENT, FIRST RESPONDERS AND ALL THE HEALTH CARE PROFESSIONALS WHO HAVE WORKED SO HARD AND SACRIFICED SO MUCH TO TRY AND KEEP US ALIVE DURING THIS PANDEMIC.

A SPECIAL SALUTE TO MY MARINE CORP'S BROTHERS AND SISTERS. YOU ARE ALL HEROES IN MY BOOK AND I AM SO PROUD TO HAVE SERVED WITH YOU. SEMPER FI.

I ALSO WANT TO GIVE PROPS TO MY DAD, WHO NOT ONLY SERVED IN THE ARMY FOR FIVE YEARS DURING WORLD WAR 1, BUT ALSO MADE THE WORLD A BETTER PLACE TO LIVE WITH SOME OF HIS DECISIONS LATER ON IN LIFE AS A CIVIL ENGINEER.

SOME PEOPLE SPENT AN ENTIRE LIFE WONDERING IF THEY MADE A DIFFERENCE. THE MARINES DON'T HAVE THAT PROBLEM.

PRESIDENT RONALD REAGAN

DO NOT ATTACT "THE FIRST MARINE DIVISION". THEY FIGHT LIKE DEVILS.

CHINESE MILITARY DIRECTIVE, (KOREA, 1951)

THE SAFEST PLACE IN KOREA WAS RIGHT BEHIND A PLATOON OF MARINES. LORD HOW THEY COULD FIGHT.

MAJOR GENERAL FRANK E. LOWE, USA; KOREA, 26 JAN. 1952

D1225764

REV. A

TABLE OF CONTENTS:

PROLOGUE:

Why did I write this book? I wrote it mainly to pay tribute to the Marines, The South, and Family. It is biographical to a degree and the first ten chapters are pretty much in Chronological order. It's also a collection of lifetime memories, facts, stories about the South, Civil Engineering, Military school, Puerto Rico, The Marine Corp's (My platoon in combat training participated in the filming of the movie "Battle Cry" at Camp Pendleton, California in 1954), about Korea, Southern people, Country and Gospel music, Hunting, Fishing, Southern Churches, Baptisms, etc. I also included some family vacation suggestions and give my opinion of Presidents, parties, and policies.

Richard J. Davis Jr.

Acknowledgement: I want to thank my son "Brian" for proofreading this book and for some of his suggestions.

Introduction:

This Book is a follow up to my previous book "Memories-The Marines, The South and Family" published last year. After I published it, My Son said Dad, you need to dig much deeper. He said and I quote "once you are gone, these stories go with you". So, to be completely honest and candid, the first ten chapters are similar to my first book (with some additions), but since then, I have added 37 pages, over six thousand words, six additional chapters and numerous photos. It is much more in depth and has new stories, new anecdotes, new facts, more history and a whole chapter of old-time legacy photos, some family vacation suggestions and three letters from me to "President Trump" and five of his signed responses.

Although, I am not exactly an activist, I have had 14 or 15 opinions published in the Cincinnati Enquirer. In chapter 15, I give my honest opinion on current events and what I think is tearing us apart as a nation.

Since I am the current Patriarch of the Davis family and the one writing this book, I guess I could be called the central character, but this is not a self-lauding autobiography. If there is anyone that I might brag on, it would be my father. I consider him to be one of the best "Civil Engineers" that ever lived (more on that later) and a real "Renaissance" man. I will introduce him and my mom (He was a "Yankee", She was a "Southern Belle"), where they were born and raised, how they met, and their relationship.

First, I will cover the period between 1935 and 1957. During that period, I Went to Military School for 4 years. We lived in "Puerto Rico" for 4-1/2 years. I spent 3 years in the Marine Corp's (10-1/2 months in Korea) and took part in the filming of the movie "Battle Cry" at Camp Pendleton, California before going to Korea. A real interesting experience.

Interspersed with all this, I will include, in my opinion, how "southern people" think, how they feel, what their general philosophy might be and how hard they had to work and struggle to survive in the old days. Many are still struggling today (particularly the coal miners). I had two uncles who were coal miners in Harlan County, Kentucky and one in Campbell County, Tennessee. I kind of have a unique perspective since we traversed back and forth between Knoxville and my Grand-Mother's house, which was about 3 miles north of LaFollette, Tenn.

Granny Long lived a hard life, did not bend till the end, and would not have had it any other way.

We Southerners are not "Deplorables" (as Hillary Clinton said) and do a lot more than just "cling to our guns and bibles" (as President Barack Obama said) and we're sure as hell not stupid (regardless of our twang).

 I guess the question I would ask, if what these people say is true, why are so many people and company's relocating to the South. I'll answer that for you. Three southern states do not have state income taxes, they have a lower cost of living, less crime, better climate, less traffic congestion, a good work ethic, delicious southern cooking, polite manners, splendid hunting & fishing, good football, good music, good people, and good-looking women. What more could you ask for in these troubled times?

I will then cover the period between 1957, and the present but will intentionally leave out family members and others complete names, places of employment, addresses, etc., because, in today's PC, Woke, Anal, Cancel Culture society, you can't be too careful. One wrong word and you can be out of a job or have some degenerate harassing you.

I don't think there is a single Marine (active, discharged or retired) who would not get a kick out of reading chapters 6 and 7. I tried to write it in a way that a lay non-military person would understand and enjoy.

So put down your Tablets, I-phones, Lattes, and biases, and read on, you might enjoy it and hopefully learn somethings you didn't already know.

It is reasonably priced, probably less than a "Hamburger and fries" in today's world, and while that's "food for your body", I hope there's maybe some "food for your soul" in this book.

Richard

Chapter 1: **My Dad (His Heartbreak and Moving Forward).**

My Dad was born in Manor, Pennsylvania (a suburb of Pittsburg) in 1894. He graduated from Carnegie institute of Technology in 1917, with a degree in Civil Engineering. He subsequently joined the Army and served from 1917 until 1922. His various postings included Panama, The Philippines, and The Siberian Expedition in Russia.

After getting out of the Army, he took a job with the West-Penn. Power Co. and went to work in the area around Davis and Thompson, West Virginia (1922 to 1927). He met and married a lady named "Avilda Thompson" and they had a baby girl (Edna June). Dad's wife died giving birth and his baby girl died seven months later from pneumonia. They are both buried in Davis, West Virginia. I have been to their graves. He was so distraught that he quit his job and took a job with the "United Fruit Co." (1927-1928). He was sent to Guatemala and did the civil engineering consistent with setting up Banana plantations, Land surveys, farm layout, irrigation, Tram locations, etc.

His next job was in Bermuda (1928-1929, Bermuda Railroad Co. Ltd.) where he did civil engineering on the first and only railroad in that "British Crown Colony". The "Bermuda Railway" operated from 1931 to 1948. In 1984, the defunct rail line's right-of-way was dedicated as the "Bermuda Railway Trail" for hiking, and for biking on some paved sections.

He went back to The West-Penn. power Co. (1929-1930) to complete some control triangulation, previously started (in Civil Engineering and surveying, that is the process of determining the location of a point by measuring only angles to it from known points at either end of a fixed baseline).

Then, it was back to work for the "United Fruit Co." in Columbia, South America, (1930-1931) doing work, like what he had done in Guatemala, except in much more depth. This time he had to do a Town-site location and layout, Railroad location and construction oversight, land surveys, farm layout, irrigation studies.

Some funny little stories (and one not to funny) about Columbia. "United Fruit Co." had bunk houses, etc., for the men to stay in when working in the jungle on these various plantations. There was a lot of monkeys, and they were a nuisance. Periodically the men would spread piles of oats around the compound, douse them with rum and the next morning the monkeys would all be laying around passed out. They would put them in sacks and throw them over the back of a mule and haul them miles away. Relative peace would reign for a few days until they found their way back.

Dad had a place on his left forefinger where a monkey had bit him, and he had a big scar on his shin. The way he got that, he was traveling through the jungle on horse-back and a big snake crossed his path. It scared the Horse and when it reared up, he fell off and suffered a compound fracture to his leg.

When they set up these camps in the jungle, they always had a clubhouse of sorts so the men could sit around and chat and have a few drinks in the evenings. Dad said they would eventually start singing. They sang great old songs like "Danny Boy", "Swanee by Al Jolson", "up a lazy river", "Mills Brothers songs", "Louie Armstrong songs", "Old man river", etc. Dad used to tell me he was what they called a "Whiskey Tenor".

RICHARD J. DAVIS SR. (MY DAD, WORLD WAR 1)

HE WAS IN THE U.S. CALVARY WHEN THIS PICTURE WAS TAKEN.

MATTIE MILDRED (LONG) DAVIS (MY MOM)

He finally made it back to Pittsburg in the early thirties (during the great depression) and his sister Edna said there was no work in that area, but she had read about a big rural electrification and flood control project starting up in Tennessee by a new government entity called the "Tennessee Valley Authority" (TVA) headquartered in Knoxville. He went down to Knoxville, and they hired Him.

The TVA started construction on Norris Dam in 1933, and Dad's first assignment was taking survey parties and surveying east from the Dam site, "up the valley" toward Middlesboro, Ky. Norris Dam is just below the confluence of the Clinch River and the Powell River. They had to determine approx. how far Norris Lake would extend and how many thousand acres it was going to cover once the Dam was completed and the locks were closed. A lot of people had to be relocated and a lot of things had to be moved, especially cemeteries. The town of "Loyston" (population approx. 70-100 people in 1935) was to be inundated by the waters of Norris Lake, requiring the relocation or demolition of schools, homes, churches, general stores, cemeteries, etc., What little remains of "The sunken city of Loyston" is now 60 to 90 feet under water, depending on the season.

They had similar challenges with all the other Dam's, Watts Bar, Douglas, Cherokee, Fontana, etc. By this time, dad had taken over the TVA's railroad design and hundreds of miles of railroad spurs had to be built or relocated, many in very mountainous terrain with excessive cuts and fills and difficult drainage considerations.

Dad spent a lot of time in LaFollette, which is near Norris Lake. He would stay at the Piedmont hotel when he was there. Once, he came driving up to the Hotel and forgot to pump the brakes on the car he was driving (you had to do that on some of the cars back then) and ran right into the side of the building. I think he was driving a "DeSoto" coupe at the time. I am not sure whether he met my mom in Knoxville or LaFollette. She was raised about 6 miles north of LaFollette on US25W. They were married and I was born in Knoxville in 1935.

Norris Dam 1937

There was a movie called "Wild River" filmed entirely in Tennessee and released in 1959 by director "Elia Kazan", which, although loosely based on two previous novels is mainly about the "Tennessee Valley Authority" building dams to produce electricity for the south and for flood control and the extreme reluctance of some people to sell their homes and property and relocate.

Dad worked for the TVA until 1944, and then took a job with a company called "James B. Sullivan consulting Engineering". They were one of the top railroad consulting firms in the country. One of His first assignments was coming to Cincinnati and totally reconfiguring the big railroad yard behind Union terminal (which he also did in several other major cities).

He next took a job with "Long Construction Co." in Puerto Rico (Nov. 1947). Their headquarters were in Darlington, South Carolina. They had already built several sub-divisions in Puerto Rico and under a U.S. government program called "operation bootstrap" they were getting ready to build an additional 10,000 concrete, single and duplex houses near San Juan. The ideal behind this was to try and build enough affordable housing to help eliminate some of the slums. They hired Dad as their chief engineer. Mom and I went to Puerto Rico in January of 1948. Dad subsequently worked in Spain, Ecuador, and Liberia. We'll cover that a little bit later.

MY DADS FATHER "OWEN JAMES DAVIS" AND HIS SECOND WIFE AFTER DAD'S MOM PASSED AWAY.

MY DADS MOTHER "SARAH ANN (SMITH) DAVIS" IN THE CENTER

I PERSONALLY THINK DADS' MOM WAS SO PRETTY.

MY DAD'S SISTER "EDNA", SHE WAS A NAVY NURSE IN WW I.

She was trapped in a submarine one time on the bottom of the ocean, but they eventually figured out the problem and were able to surface.

Chapter 2: Knoxville and LaFollette (Early Memories).

We drove to Pittsburg in 1936 to see Grandpa Davis. He was on his death bed and wanted to see his only Grandson (Me) before he passed away. He was a Mining Engineer who immigrated from Wales thru Ellis Island in the 1880's. He passed away shortly thereafter, but we did not go back for the funeral. A trip from Knoxville to Pittsburg in those days was very arduous because this was long before the interstate highway system was built.

Dad was 16 years old when his mother passed away (1910) and he then spent a lot of time with his aunt. He used to laugh about the "lima bean sandwiches" that she prepared for him and his cousin to take to school. It was a far cry from the good southern cooking he would get, once he relocated to Dixie.

We lived in Knoxville from 1935 until 1948 and went back and forth to LaFollette frequently and if dad couldn't go, mom and I would ride the "Greyhound bus" (it's about 42 miles). In those days, the Greyhound bus would stop and pick up or drop off people about anywhere. "Granny Long" now lived about 3 miles north of LaFollette on US25W, because the original home place which was about 6 miles north of town had burned down. "Grandpa Long" had passed away in 1929.

Dad worked overseas almost exclusively, and "Granny Long's" place was always their stop-over between overseas assignments. They finally bought her a place in LaFollette between dad's second assignment in Ecuador (around 1959-60) and before going to Liberia for two years. His final overseas assignment.

The place Granny had built after the original homeplace burned was initially only two rooms and a porch, but through the years, dad, with a little help, added on two more rooms, a summer porch, etc. I don't think she had electricity until probably the late forties, and she never had indoor plumbing or water. We got our water from a hollow up the road, and when it dried up, we had to go down the road, maybe a quarter mile or so, and when that dried up, we had to go to a spring which was located right outside of LaFollette. We would hire a taxi and take a bunch of gallon jugs with us. Cab fare to town at that time was $1.00. That spring still runs fresh and ice cold today.

Granny was a hard worker. She planted a big garden every year and what wasn't eaten immediately, was either canned, dried, or stored in a root cellar. We picked a lot of blackberries and apples for making jelly. Occasionally, she would make a little "blackberry wine". She usually had a hog to kill and be processed each fall and would render lard and sometimes make lye soap (the "lye" was a caustic substance derived from wood ashes; a chemical reaction occurs when lye is mixed with oil, creating soap). Chickens were always present, and she always had a few running loose in the yard. They roosted in trees at night. Her appliances consisted of an ice box and a wood burning cook stove. People in the country were very self-sufficient and about all they had to buy were the staples, such as matches, sugar, salt, black pepper, flour, coffee, pinto beans, coal oil, cornmeal and maybe milk and butter (if they didn't have a cow). "Prince albert in a can", "cigarette papers" or some "Garretts sweet snuff", a little hard candy, orange slices and some "moon pies" and "RC cola" might have also been on the shopping list.

WILLIAM BURKE LONG
c 1909, AGE 40

1869-1929

Grandpa Long

ANNIE WICKS LONG
c 1954, AGE 72
B 1882 d 1971, AGE 89

1882-1971

Granny Long

The "Blue Bird" (a grocery truck) came by each week. They sold everything from groceries to chicken feed. The day the "Blue Bird" ran was a big deal, because Granny always bought me a little treat. The ice man also came by each week.

What was Granny's house like at Christmas time? Well, everybody had a stocking with something like this in it. An apple, an orange, maybe a few nuts, some hard candy, a little bit of change, etc.

Granny only had sleeping space for about five people in the beds, so us kids would make what we called "pallets" and slept on the floor.

A lot of country folks had "feather beds" or "straw ticks" back in those days. This was basically a cotton or linen bag filled with feathers or straw.

Life on the farm and in rural communities, in what, "I'll call the good old days" meant hard work and frugal habits. A lot of families could not afford store bought clothes, so they would take flour sacks and feed sacks with printed designs on them and make dresses, aprons, dish towels, curtains, quilts, diapers, bonnets, pillows (filled with feathers), etc. My Granny and most other women living in the south at that time always wore a dress. If they went shopping, visiting, or to church, they wore a dress, and if they were working in the garden, hoeing corn, etc., they wore a dress, an apron and usually a hat or bonnet.

Me and some of the other kids who lived down the road would dam up a section of the creek and create a swimming hole about every summer. I took many baths down below Granny's house in that same creek because of the scarcity of water.

Granny used to make me walk up and down the high-way or railroad (L and N Railroad) and pick up coal that had fallen from the coal trucks or rail cars. Also, if a truck wrecked and spilled its load, we had to trek back and forth carrying buckets full of whatever had been spilt. One time it was a load of "shelled corn", which she wanted to feed her hogs. Another time, a truck full of "frozen chickens" wrecked (on top of Peabody Mountain) and people in the area spent hours in their cars or on foot carrying chickens' home to put in their freezers or ice boxes.

Dad made me a sling shot one time when I was about 7 or 8 years old, and he decided to try it out. We were standing on the side porch, and he shot it down through the back yard. Lo and behold, he killed one of Granny's big hens. She saw it and threatened to kill Him. You see, she thought a lot of her hens, but not so much of my dad. He was a "Yankee" and Granny who was born in 1882, wasn't too fond of "Yankees" or "Carpetbaggers".

She used to tell me a story about a little chicken call "Hopping Dick". You see "Hopping Dick" was crippled and a Yankee soldier (during the civil war) came on this southern farm and caught poor little "Hopping Dick" and was going to eat him. The southern ladies last words were "Poor little Hopping Dick, the Yankee's got you now". I bet that story goes back to civil war times, (even old honest "Abe Lincoln" might have known that story).

I remember my mom getting mad at my dad and calling him a "Damn Hook Nose Yankee Bastard". You see, dad's nose had been broken several times and Mom (being a southern Belle) just felt that referencing his nose and his "Yankee" heritage was appropriate when he pissed her off.

My mom had five sisters and two brothers. The only one that stayed permanently in Campbell County, Tenn. was her older brother John (a coal miner). Sometimes, Dad and John would drink a little "Tennessee shine" and dad would hold a pet cream can in his hand and John would shoot it out with a twenty-two rifle. Thank God, he was a good shot. I have some other stories about John and his friends that we will talk about a little later.

We all loved the "Royal Pool Room" in LaFollette. At that time, women did not go inside. You could get two of the best Hot Dogs in the world and a six-ounce coke for 25 cents. It's still in business and women are now allowed in (nothings sacred anymore, just kidding girls). If you are ever thru LaFollette, Tennessee on 25W, do not pass it by. It's been in business since 1933.

There was a "Beer Joint" (that's what people in Tennessee called them at the time) just a few hundred feet south of Granny's house on 25W and the owner "Rhoda Minton" sold beer and bootleg whiskey. Beer was legal and whiskey was not. She would hide her whiskey across the highway (not on her property) and send an employee over to get it when someone wanted to buy some. I just happened to be prowling around in the woods one day and ran upon Rhoda's stash, so Granny and I confiscated it and took it three miles up the road and sold it to her sister (who also ran a beer joint). We were just trying to rid old "Rhoda" of her sinful ways.

Meanwhile, back in Knoxville, I remember the time mom came in and dad and I were in the floor breaking my piggy bank to get money to go the "Ringling Brothers and Barnum Bailey Circus", "The greatest show on earth". Times were hard as the country was just coming out of the Great Depression.

Another time a "traveling Rodeo" came to Knoxville and they signed a contract with the city to have it at the baseball stadium. They had a bull named "Big Cid" and if you could stay on him for 8 seconds, you would win some prize money. Well, when the rodeo was over and they were getting ready to leave town, Knoxville wouldn't give the owner his full share of the money because they said he had messed up the turf on the ball field. I'll never forget the owner saying and I quote "I might not have gotten all my money, but by-God they didn't ride "Big Cid".

Another funny memory was the "Cas Walker" signs around Knoxville. You see "Cas Walker" was a local entrepreneur who owned a bunch of grocery stores. His signs used to say, "You might beat our prices, but you can't beat our meat" (ha). He also had a radio and TV show. This was "Dolly Parton's" first exposure to television and radio. By the way, I consider "Dolly" to be a national treasure.

When I was around five or six years old, the TVA transferred dad to Chattanooga for a while and we shared a house with another couple named "the Walls". The man's name was Harry, and they had a son they called "little Harry". Well one day, Harry was swinging "little Harry" back and forth in a blanket and one end slipped loose and "little Harry" hit the wall. Harry said and I quote "Damn Dick, I believe I've killed little Harry". "Little Harry" was ok, but dad would get so tickled when he told that story.

World war II started on Dec. 7th, 1941, That's the day that the Japanese bombed Pearl Harbor. I am not going to retell the history of World War II, because there have been many books written about it, but I might point out a few things that the younger generation might not know. About everything was rationed during the war (gas, sugar, coffee, meat, nylons, etc.) It was amazing how the American people came together to support the war effort. Many young men went off to war and the women stayed home and worked in the factories. One of the popular images used on posters during the war was of a young woman they called "Rosie the Riveter". The numbers are not exact, but somewhere in the vicinity of 60 to 85 million people died worldwide (US and Allies) fighting to keep us free from tyranny. The Japanese surrendered on Sept. 2nd, 1945.

One little thing that I found interesting. Hideki Tojo was Japan's Prime Minister and army minister during world WWII. He was arrested and imprisoned at the end of the war. While in prison, he had a dental problem and the American dentist who made his new dentures (unbeknownst) to Tojo engraved "Remember Pearl Harbor" (in morse code) inside his dentures. Tojo was executed on Dec. 23rd, 1948.

The Troop Train accident near Jellico, Tennessee (July 6th, 1944):

A terrible accident took place just South of Jellico, Tennessee on the "L and N" railroad on July 6th, 1944. A troop train traveling south with 1,006 young Army recruits on board derailed and 37 young men died and 74 more were injured. The topography in that area is basically highway "US25W" hugs the mountain on the west side of a deep gorge (with a river running thru it) and the railroad sits above the gorge on the other side. There are differing views on what happened, some say the train was improperly loaded and was oscillating, some say it was traveling too fast, but regardless, the "Engine, Tender and four cars" jumped the track and were either in the water or hanging down the side of the hill. There were bodies strewn everywhere, some in the water, some were trapped, some burned, some drowned. Soon as the word got out, people from all around the area started showing up to try and help, including two of my uncles (John and Bill Long). "Block and Tackles" were rigged up to help get these poor injured men up the fifty-foot or so embankment to the highway, where they were put in cars, trucks, school buses, etc. and taken to five small towns in the area that had some sort of medical facility. This wreck was the second worst stateside tragedy to occur during World War II.

Mom was an air raid warden during World War II and when the sirens went off at night, she had to walk the neighborhood and tell people to turn off their lights. Try that these days. Dad would naturally get mad when he had to walk her route.

Early 1940'S, going to get ice cream in a 40'S Pontiac and we all sang "the Hut-Sut song". The first line was "Hut-Sut Rawlson on the Rillerah and a Brawla, Brawla Sooit". A big hit in the 40'S. It is described on "Google" as a novelty song with nonsense lyrics. Sort of like a lot of this Rap right now. It was featured in three movies.

The last place we lived in Knoxville, before going to Puerto Rico was close to "The University of Tennessee" and I used to ride my bicycle over and watch General Robert Neyland's "Vols" practice that old "single wing attack" at Shields-Watkins field (which is now Neyland stadium). General Neyland's record at Tennessee was 173 wins in 216 games. Six undefeated seasons, seven conference championships and four national championships.

Chapter 3: Junior Military Academy (1943-1947).

I went to "Junior Military Academy" (near Cookeville, Tennessee) from the middle of the fourth grade until the middle of the eighth grade. They had classes from Tuesday thru Saturday (don't ask me why). We were off on Sunday and Monday. I was a drummer in the little drum and bugle Corp's.

The school had a farm down the road with 6 or 8 horses and we would go get them on Sundays and Mondays and bring them to campus and the cadets would take turns riding.

We had two cadets from Panama. I would guess there was a couple of years difference in their ages. One day, the younger one was sitting behind the schoolhouse and a bullet hit him right in the stomach. He was seriously injured and almost died. The school was out in the country, so they never found out who fired the shot. It could have just been someone target shooting or hunting.

I would sometimes slip off Campus and buy stuff at a grocery truck that came around weekly. One of the things I used to buy was "Spam" and I still like it to this day. Hey, it is the national meat of Hawaii, because it's about all they could get during World War II.

Sometimes in the fall, dad would ride the train from Knoxville to Cookeville on Fridays and spend the night at the "Shanks Hotel" and we would go to the "Tennessee Tech." football games on Saturday. I always liked to go to the "B and B" restaurant and eat hamburger steak (a southern staple).

Major Roy DeBerry was the owner and headmaster of "Junior Military Academy", and he also drank excessively. I was standing outside the shower room one day (semi-naked) waiting to take a shower and he happened to walk by. He heard me tell the kid in the shower to save me some "Damn" hot water. Well, he took offense to my mildly bad language. He reached into the room next door, got a wooden broom, and beat me mercilessly with it. I had terrible bruises when I went home to Knoxville for Christmas vacation, so mom pulled me from school, and we went to "Puerto Rico" in January of 1948. I know the first thought that comes to mind is, why didn't mom sue him. Well, dad was already in Puerto Rico, she had no support system, little money and Major DeBerry was a big man in Putnam County, Tennessee. Her chances of winning a lawsuit were slim and none.

If any of your relatives are still alive, I hope they read this, you overbearing old bastard.

I do believe though in giving credit where credit is due. The discipline that I learned at "Junior Military Academy" served me well later in life (in Catholic High school in Puerto Rico and the Marine Corp's).

Cadet Richard J Davis Jr, Left photo with cape. Right photo is with one of my fellow cadets in the drum and bugle Corp's. I played the drums.

Chapter 4: Puerto Rico (1948-1952, 1964)

Enjoyable experience for the most part. I went to Catholic high school in Rio Piedras (Colegio San Jose) for 3 of the 4 years. Although we weren't Catholic, the Priests made me go to Mass every morning.

I played a lot of golf in my spare time, softball, went to the beach, etc. I once played several rounds of golf with a famous Cuban singer (Miguelito Valdes). He happened to be at "Fort Buchanan", near San Juan, where I played most of the time and was looking for a partner. He had a monster hit in the Latin community back in the fifty's called "Babalu". Singer/songwriter "Bobby Capo" was very popular at that time in Puerto Rico and "Perez Prado" had just introduced "Que Rico El Mambo" and "Mambo #5" leading to "Mambo mania".

In my humble opinion, the work that dad did in Puerto Rico was nothing short of amazing. I am not exactly sure how many houses or apartment buildings were eventually built, but the original statement said 575 houses at "Ramey Air Force Base" and approx. 10,000 concrete single and duplex houses were to be built, mostly near San Juan. His company also built several Apartment buildings. The area where we lived was called "Caparra Heights", had about 500 houses, and was already built when we got there. The area that was under construction while we were there was called "Puerto Nuevo" and I believe they had built about 4300 houses when we came back to the states. At one point they were completing 13 houses per day. Long Construction Co. was selling them for $3,995 dollars each. Dad had responsibility for all the civil engineering. Sub-division layout, streets, sidewalks, sewers, Water lines, power, grading operations, etc., with nothing more than 10 survey parties, a drawing board, and a slide rule. There was no computers, Google Earth, drones, or GPS back then.

A partial view of Puerto Nuevo Subdivision near San Juan.

President Truman came to Puerto Rico for a little visit and inspection tour in Feb. of 1948 and his motorcade came to Caparra Heights, where we lived, and went around the traffic circle in front of our house. At that time, it was a patch of weeds and had not yet been landscaped.

One night my dad and I were sitting on the front porch and a Puerto Rican kid from down the street kept riding around in front of our house, on his bike, and he kept calling me "cobarde" (coward). Finally, my dad said, "why don't you go out there and knock the shit out of him". I did just that, I walked out and knocked him off his bicycle and he jumped up and pulled a knife on me and I in turn, jerked out my switch blade. It was going to get ugly, but my mom came running out, grabbed both our knifes and threw them over in the weeds in the traffic circle. I went back to Puerto Rico in the late 80'S and that traffic circle now has a large tree growing in it. I wonder if the landscapers found my switch blade.

Long Construction Co. issued shotguns to all employees the year (Nov. 1950) two Puerto Rican activists went to Washington, DC and attempted to assassinate

President Truman. Tension was very high at that time between Americans and Puerto Rican's, so we had to be extra careful.

Me with my mom and dad, Puerto Rico, c.1952

This is the kind of car I learned how to drive in when I was sixteen years old. A very large 1946 Buick, 4 door sedan.

Note: Puerto Rico, c.1952, I had parallel bars and weights just to the right and for you history buffs, that's a Columbia bicycle sitting there. I worked out every day to try and keep those Puerto Ricans from whipping my ass, which they never did.

There was a boxing gymnasium at the "Sixto Escobar" sports complex in San Juan and a friend and I used to go there and box occasionally. There was also a baseball stadium, and I would sometimes go to the "Puerto Rican winter league" baseball games. At that time, each Puerto Rican team was allowed to have five foreign players. I remember an American player named "Willard (home run) Brown" who would come to Puerto Rico and play every winter. The "Cincinnati Reds" also used to do part of their spring training in Puerto Rico.

The house we lived in was all concrete construction with a flat roof and did not have windows, just screens and metal shutters. The reason I am pointing this out is because they have Hurricanes quite frequently in Puerto Rico (as we have seen in the last couple of years), and this was a safer way to go. I had a little green lizard who lived in my bedroom, and they were great for killing flies and mosquitos, so I just left him alone and he left me alone. We also had a banana tree in our back yard and a lime tree right outside the kitchen door.

We always had a maid, so my mom didn't have a lot to do. She was an artsy, craftsy type person, so she normally kept busy with art lessons, dance lessons, acting classes, plays, bridge and canasta clubs, painting, etc.

Vendors used to come around our neighborhood with push carts and they sold things like loaves of Italian style bread, Bananas, Plantains, Avocados, Mangos, Guayaba, Pineapples, papaya, etc.

Cockfighting was legal when we lived in Puerto Rico and our next-door neighbor had several cages next to his house with fighting cocks in them. There were many cockfighting arenas around the island at that time.

Dad made me drive him about everywhere we went together. Sometimes we went to a famous bar and restaurant in old San Juan called "La Mallorquina" and Dad would roll the dice with the Bartender to see whether he had to pay or not. It was either double or nothing.

Some other places we went were Old San Juan, Luquillo beach, Isla Verde beach, (amongst many others), El Morro castle, El Yunque rain forest (hiking, waterfalls, swimming, backpack camping, wildlife, etc.), Parque de Bombas in Ponce (an ornamental firehouse), The Bacardi Rum Distillery, La Parguera Bioluminescent Bay near Lajas, (the bay's glowing effect is made possible by micro-organisms called "dinoflagellates" which emit a short burst of light when agitated). It's neat to go out in a boat or kayak at night and see all these little streaks of light in the water. "Rincon" is a great place to surf and if you are into "caving", you would enjoy the "Cavernas del Rio Camuy" which is the third largest cave network on the planet.

I remember the day we were playing softball in the vacant parking lot across from where we lived, and I kept fouling balls into this guy's yard up the street. He called the cops and they decided to arrest me. Puerto Rican cops did not like Americans very much. When they tried to arrest me, I shoved one of the cops and took off down the street to our house. I got dad's shotgun and sat down in the living room. They came to our house, but never entered. Long Construction Co. (dad's employer) gave the cop's an empty house to use as a temporary police station after that incident, which I guess kept me out of jail.

My first summer job was as a Plumbers helper, putting the hot and cold-water lines in the Darlington Apartment building (Edificio Darlington) which dad's company was building in Santurce (a suburb of San Juan).

Since I now had a little spending money of my own, I would go into Santurce or San Juan on Friday nights to a bar, sit on a stool, thinking I was cool, and maybe drink a couple of Cuba Libre's (Bacardi Rum and coke). One night, the U.S. Navy shore patrol came in and wanted to see my papers. I recall telling them that I didn't have to show them any papers, I was a civilian.

Adolph Rupp brought the 1950/1951, Kentucky basketball team to Puerto Rico for a series of exhibition games. I went to several of the games and went to the "Condado" Beach Hotel in Isla Verde and got to talk to Coach Rupp. I had bought an 8 x 10 glossy at one of the games and got His and all the players autographs. He asked me where I was from, and I said Tennessee. He then "cracked that they always beat us at Basketball" and "I cracked back that we always beat them at Football". It was funny watching those big, tall basketball players frolicking around the pool with those little 5-foot-tall Puerto Rican girls.

Dad came out of retirement and went back to Puerto Rico in 1964. Long Construction Company contacted him and asked him to go back to supervise the pile driving portion of a parking garage near Edificio Darlington. Dad explained the process to me once for driving piles to the "point of refusal". He was one hell of an Engineer, and his hard work and creativity survives today, seventy years later.

Adios Puerto Rico y Buena suerte (goodbye Puerto Rico and good luck).

Ricardo

Chapter 5: Richmond, Va. (1953).

Mom and I flew home from Puerto Rico to New York in August of 1952. We stayed at the Lexington hotel in Manhattan for several days and did all the touristy things. We then rode a Greyhound bus home from New York to Granny Long's house in LaFollette. Dad followed soon after.

He then took a job with a company in Richmond, Virginia and we moved there in January of 1953 and all he ever said about his job was that they were working on something being built in Iceland. I'm sure he had a security clearance at that time and would not talk about it. I got a job at a company called "Crawford Mfg. Co." as a shipping clerk.

Each day I had to walk from the shipping dept. to the office with paperwork, and I went through a room full of Seamstresses who always flirted and made wise cracks. Well, this guy started giving me a hard time about it (I think he was jealous). One day, I just stopped and decked him. It wasn't long before I got a call to come up to the Managers office and my first thought was "I'm fired". Lo and behold when I got there, the Boss shook my hand, gave me a raise, and said that "smart ass" had needed that for a long time. What that "smart ass" never knew; I was dating one of those sweet little seamstresses at the time.

I used to go to the races at the "Richmond Raceway". The hot car back then was the "Hudson Hornet" (1951-1954).

1951 Hudson Hornet race car.

Not long after that, I departed Richmond rather abruptly after some Cop came to our house and told mom I had been flirting with his wife and he would be back the next day. I didn't know flirting was against the law (besides, I was innocent, He-He). Anyway, I caught the "big Grey Dog" to Tennessee and Granny Long's house the next morning.

I spent the summer at Granny's house after leaving Richmond. Mom kept calling and said that I needed to start college in September or get a job. I did neither and joined the Marine Corps in Knoxville on Sept. 15, 1953. The two Marine recruiters who signed me up made the Marine Corp's sound pretty glamorous (They both had nice tans, I think from "sunbathing" on top of the post office). They said once I completed basic training, I'd probably be somewhere like Southern California laying on the beach. Boy was that a bunch of BS. I was on my way to Korea about 9 months later.

The recruits who joined in Knoxville were sent shortly thereafter to Nashville. In Nashville you received your preliminary physical, took a test, signed some papers and were sworn in. You were told to report to the train station that night for the trip to South Carolina. Once in South Carolina, you were put on a bus and taken to Parris Island.

Me on my dad's 51 Ford

Richmond, Va. c.1953

Chapter 6: United States Marine Corps (1953-1956).

The Marine Corp's, what can I say? You either love it or hate it. We arrived at "Parris Island", late at night to start basic training and from the minute you stepped off the bus onto those yellow "footprints" and those drill instructors start screaming at you and calling you names, like maybe, "Girls and Maggots". You are sure that you have passed away and gone straight to hell. I know some things have changed, but the physical and mental abuse back in the fifty's almost took your breath away and many guys couldn't take it and dropped out.

The Marine Corps has the whole process down to a science. Their concept is to break everyone down to the most basic form of life (almost like a newborn baby) and then rebuild you in their image. One of the first things they do is shave your head to rid everyone of any vestiges of vanity that they might have. Every minute is scheduled, from the time they roust you out at five in the morning, until lights out at night.

Since I was in the Marines from 1953 until 1956, I'm sure many things have changed, but boot camp was basically, a twelve-week process. Orientation the first week (they issued your rifle, M1 Garand 30-06, your gear, physicals, dental checkup, shots, etc.) and you are then assigned to your platoon and start the training regime. Marching, physical conditioning, classes on different subjects, gas mask training, obstacle courses, mess duty, two weeks at the rifle range (snapping in and qualifying), KP, orientation on different weapons, throwing live Grenades, inspections, etc. It is something else when we were "in formation", and rifles were being inspected. The recruit is at port arms and the "DI" stops in front of you and you don't know whether he is going to inspect your rifle or not. If he brings his hand up to grab your rifle, you better turn it loose at exactly the right time and it better not hit the ground.

Also learning how to march properly is something else. When you first get there, for the "DI", it was like herding cats, but by-God, by the time you're ready to graduate, everyone is in step, and every heel is hitting that "Damn hot South Carolina asphalt" at the same time. I remember the "Drill Instructors" cadence and I quote, "Heel, Heel, Heel, give me your left, your right, your left". We were looking and sounding awesome.

Some funny little side bars. Parris Island has billions of sand fleas, but when we were in formation, we were not allowed to swat them, no matter how much they chewed on us. The drill instructors always said that the fleas had to eat also.

The Marine Corp's also has a basic philosophy that every Marine is first and foremost a Rifleman. In basic training, you are not allowed to call your rifle, a gun. The penalty for doing so was that they made you walk up and down the street holding your rifle in one hand and a certain part of the male anatomy in the other hand and saying and I quote "this is my rifle, this is my gun, this is for fighting, this is for fun". Crass, but effective. Thank God, I never called my rifle, a gun.

PFC RICHARD DAVIS, PARRIS ISLAND c.1953

On graduation day, all the graduating platoons assemble at the parade ground for a final review. As you march past the reviewing stand and the band strikes up the "Marine Corp's Hymn", well it just doesn't get any better than that. The DI'S part in the process was over. That's when I started to realize, by toughing it out, I had made the right decision.

Graduation day at Parris Island. I was in the fourth row up, fourth from the right.

We next flew from South Carolina to Los Angeles and were bussed to "Camp Pendleton" to start combat training. We were interrupted for four weeks to take part in the filming of the movie "Battle cry". The sequences that our platoon(s) were in, are filmed at Camp Pendleton, other parts were filmed at San Diego, Vieques Island, Puerto Rico, and Hollywood. It was an interesting experience. It starred Van Heflin, Aldo Ray, Tab Hunter, James Whitmore, Dorothy Malone, etc. The combat scenes were not filmed at Pendleton. The scenes, we mostly took part in were inspections, a 60-mile forced march, marching in formation, Billeting in squad tents, etc. Colonel Huxley (Van Heflin) was our battalion Commander in the movie, and we were called "Huxley's Harlots", but in "Leon Uris" book, they were called "Huxley's Whores", but because of censorship considerations, at the time, they changed that in the movie.

We were filming a scene one day and it was supposed to be raining, so the film crew set up sprinklers to our right and as we marched by, they turned them on, and we just kept getting wetter and wetter. Someone said "cut" and "Aldo Ray" just kept marching, and I remember him saying and I quote "Damn, I was supposed to drop out as soon as we passed the camera and get ready for the next scene," so he dropped out and started running down the road.

Colonel Huxley had a competition with another Battalion Commander about who's unit could complete a 60-mile forced march the quickest. There was one scene where our unit was resting, and the other unit was passing by in 2-1/2 ton trucks. We were told by film director "Raoul Walsh" to give them the finger as they went by. This was considered risqué in 1954. My how things have changed.

One of the background theme songs for "Battle Cry" is "Honey Babe" and we used to sing it sometimes when we marched.

My Marine Brothers and Sisters might remember this verse and I quote: "I don't want a Bar Honey, I don't want a Bar Babe, I don't want a Bar, I just want a candy bar, Honey, oh Baby of mine, give me your left, your right, your left".

The reason most Marines did not want to be the "Bar" man was because they weigh 19.4 lbs. and got damn heavy on a long hike.

The "Bar" was "Clyde Champion Barrow's" favorite weapon (of the infamous duo "Bonnie and Clyde") and Bonnie's favorite weapon was a Remington semi-automatic model 11 shotgun. Clyde liked the M1918 "Bar" (Browning automatic rifle) because of its rapid-fire capabilities. It was chambered for a 30-06 Springfield cartridge, had a 20 round detachable magazine, and could fire at a rate of 500 to 650 rounds per minute.

We completed combat training and not long after, we were taken to San Diego and put aboard the "SS COLLINS" (a merchant ship) for the 17-day trip to Korea. We made stops in Kobe and Sasebo, Japan on the way. When the Korean war ended, there was an Armistice, but never a Peace Treaty. When we got off the ship in Inchon, South Korea, there was a "Russian" soldier on the dock counting every Marine who disembarked. Evidently in the Armistice agreement, we were allowed to have a certain number of replacements entering and leaving South Korea with each monthly draft.

We then went to a transitional area called "Ascom city" (near Inchon) for a few days, until they decided which units around the country we were to be assigned to. This was done according to your "MOS" (Military occupational specialty) and the needs of the different units. I was a truck driver (3531) and was assigned to the 4.2 Mortar co, 5th Marine Regiment, 1ST Marine Division, whose camp was about 20 miles north of Seoul.

There were seven of us from what they called the "43rd Draft" sent to the same company. Our company consisted of about 160 to 180 men. The area was relatively small, a tent for the CO, one for the Lieutenants, one for the Top Sargent and platoon Sargent's, twelve-man squad tents for the rest of the company, an office tent, two tents for the "washy women", two for the slop chute (beer hall) and Navy medics, a shed for the generator (a modified jeep engine), some storage and a Quonset hut for the mess hall. The open area in the center was used for formations and parking for our nine vehicles and trailers. We had three jeeps, three 3/4-ton trucks, three 2-1/2 ton trucks and nine trailers.

There was a Headquarters platoon and three mortar platoons, each with four mortars. An assembled 4.2-inch mortar weighed approx. 333 lbs. and fired a shell that was 4.2 inches in diameter and 21 inches long. Maximum range was 4,400 yards.

The battle at the "Chosin Reservoir" was an extremely tough, but important part of the "First Marine Divisions" Korean war history:

The "Bloody Chosin Reservoir" campaign by the 120,000 Chinese soldiers was directed mainly against the 30,000 men of the "First Marine Division" and "the 31st Regimental Combat Team" (which was virtually annihilated). The fighting was brutal, in bitter cold temperatures, 36 degrees below zero at times. Tens of thousands of young Americans and Chinese were locked in eye-to-eye, hand-to-hand combat in the desolate, freezing mountains surrounding the Chosin Reservoir. The death toll soared. Even men with minor wounds or injuries frequently died. If you stopped moving, you froze.

The Marines were also in dire need of 60mm mortar shells. The radio code name for 60mm shells was "tootsie Rolls". When the air drop was finally made, they opened the crates, and they contained thousands of "Tootsie Rolls". It wasn't the shells they so badly needed, but the troops soon discovered that if they softened them in their mouth, they made a great sealant for fuel lines, manifolds, bullet holes, etc. The chocolatey goo quickly froze in the cold air and helped repair their equipment. They also provided them with badly needed nourishment.

The Chinese did force the Marines to evacuate the Reservoir, but in a deliberate retrograde movement that has become one of the most-storied exploits in Marine Corps lore, the Marines turned and fought their way down a winding, treacherous, snow packed road to Hungnam, a north Korean port 70 miles away. Through extraordinary willpower, exceptional war-fighting skills, and countless acts of valor, Marines and soldiers escaped the Chosin trap.

By the time the US forces, with thousands of refugees in tow, reached the evacuation beaches, nearly 6000 Americans were dead or missing, and thousands more were wounded. None of the men who survived the horrific battle would ever be the same. Today they are called "The Chosin Few".

God bless them all, those who made it out and those who did not.

"Reckless", the famous Marine Corp's war horse was in the fifth Marine Regiment (Recoilless Rifle Platoon, 5th Marine Regiment, 1st Marine Division). Her bravery under fire and assistance to the Marines in combat is legendary. During combat she would carry shells (by herself, in a backpack) up to the front lines and sometimes return with dead or injured Marines strapped on her back. She even knew how to hunker down (take cover) when there was incoming enemy fire. She was wounded twice and received two purple hearts. Reckless was brought from Korea to Camp Pendleton, California in the fall of 1954, where she lived out the rest of her life. She had four foals while at Camp Pendleton. Her foals were named "Fearless", "Dauntless" and "Chesty". Her last foal, a filly died a month after birth. The name "Chesty" was after "General Chesty Puller" (the most decorated Marine of all time). He was one of the few Marines ever allowed to ride Reckless. She was a staff Sargent when she passed away in May of 1968. They have a life size statue of her at the "Semper Fidelis memorial park" (at the National Museum of the Marine Corp's) near Quantico, Virginia. Amazing little Mongolian Filly. Many books have been written about her.

RECKLESS (A TRUE MARINE HERO)

Note: Reckless getting her staff Sargent stripes, c.1959.

"She wasn't a horse; she was a Marine"

Our vehicles had no heaters and were cold as hell in the winter. My main job was usually seven trips, per day, to the "water point" to get water for the "washy women" and the mess hall. The beer runs to an Army warehouse for the "slop chute" was a nice little sidebar. My buddy and I would always test the product on our way back to make sure it was ok for general consumption. Occasionally, I had to make a trip to Seoul or Inchon on business, or to pick up/deliver troops, as new drafts arrived. We sometimes had what they called "red alert's". That was when the North Koreans would start moving their troops, tanks, big guns, etc. around and we had to move out fast to our defensive positions, which was basically a fox hole on the side of a hill somewhere. We usually spent the night and about froze our "cajones" off.

Standing next to our tent in a snowstorm and that's Me, Samson (Cajun) and Lawhorn (cowboy) congratulating Eduardo (Wetback) on getting a promotion.

One of our Choppers, Korea, winter of 1954-1955

I would also take prisoners to the "First Marine Division Brig.", From time to time. That's where they got to practice making big rocks into little rocks.

I remember three instances when I took guys to the brig. One was a big guy, who used to buy a case of "Aqua Velva" aftershave lotion every payday and get stoned on it. One night, he went up to the top Sargent's tent and called him out to fight. Sarge came out and let's just say straightened him out and then after he was disciplined, I had the pleasure of taking him to the brig. Another instance was when a drunk Puerto Rican (Perez) put a loaded 45 (Colt 1911) to my head and threatened to kill me. I'm sure I said something to piss him off. I also had the pleasure of taking him to the brig. Last, but not least, we had a guy who was practicing his "fast draw" and shot himself in the foot. He went to the brig. For damaging Government property (His foot).

Another funny little remembrance, the Two "Navy medics" assigned to our unit got two gallons of alcohol each month for medicinal purposes and they would use it to make "Screw Drivers". I don't know what they would have done for alcohol in an emergency (ha).

Our main cook was a guy from "Jersey" named Chambers. We had a Sergeant that no one liked named O'Neill. One night Sgt. O'Neill was on duty and went to the mess hall about four in the morning to get a cup of coffee. Chambers was kneading dough to bake bread and there was a piece of steel wool laying on the countertop. He intentionally knocked it behind the counter and said to O'Neill, Damn sarge, I knocked that steel wool into my dough, and he just kept right on kneading. O'Neill got a funny look on his face and said he sure as hell wasn't eating any bread that next day. Chambers would tell that story and laugh like hell. When I remembered this story, I thought about "Kramer" (on Seinfeld) when he was kneading dough at the Bagel shop and dropped his chewing gum into the Bagel dough and got fired.

We had two dogs that were smart enough to always stay in our compound. One of them eventually died and the washy women were in a big fuss about who was going to take the carcass home to eat. I remember Sarge telling one of the guys to get a shovel and take it up in the woods and bury it.

About once a month, they had everyone fall out in formation before daylight. The Sgt. and one of the medics went down each row with a flash-light and each man had to expose himself and be checked for STD'S. It was called a "short arm inspection", embarrassing.

The guys in the motor pool kind of reminded me of the TV show "Mash". Our squad leader was Eduardo Lara (wetback), Gaglione (gag), a whop from Jersey, Sipes (scrounge) He was good at getting things, Goodman (skid), the wimpy little guy, Samson (Cajun), Talbot (piss tube), Lawhorn (cowboy), etc. We kind of ran the show, we had the wheels.

I remember "Gag" getting drunk and ranting (in his best Jersey dialect) about his girlfriend back in "Joisy". He would always call her a "whure" and say she was back in "Joisy" letting other guys have their way with her. That is not what he really said, but I have cleaned it up considerably.

Talbot (piss tube) got his nickname because he got drunk one night and we found him the next morning, asleep, draped around one of the "urinal tubes" that they had around our Camp.

A guy named "Buck Marler" was our barber and he also took care of the modified Jeep engine that served as our only source of electricity. One night a week, we would have movies in the mess hall and invariably the engine would start missing. We would all start hollering, and old "Buck" would have to run across the compound to get it going.

Here's a funny little story about Lawhorn (Cowboy). I guess he was getting kind of "backed up", so he came to me one day and asked if I would put him in the back of my truck (my truck had a canvas cover), drive him down to the adjacent village, pick up one of the "female entrepreneurs", park somewhere, and wait on him to "tear off a strip" and then drop her off on the way back. I said quote "are you fucking crazy", the MP'S check any vehicle that they see parked. I finally agreed to do it, but told him, we had to keep moving. The road was rough, but as far as I know, everything worked out ok. I assume He was able to stay in the saddle, after all, he was an Oklahoma Cowboy and had ridden bucking broncs. Yeehaw!

"Junior" was a Korean Guy from the village who did miscellaneous chores around our Camp during the day and was a "Pimp" at night. He would show up with "Susie", a couple of nights a week (somewhere around the perimeter of our compound) and they had a thriving business going. They were making a hell of a lot more money than we were.

I was leaving the Compound one day and when I stopped to turn onto the main road, I saw "Susie" washing her hair in a drainage ditch and started laughing. She called me a "Son of a Bitch". Damn Susie, that wasn't very polite.

I slipped down to the adjacent village (Munsani) one night to drink a little Japanese "Asahi Beer". Well, I hadn't been there long until the top Sargent showed up. We sat around with the local's drinking beer for a while and when we walked back to the compound, the sentry (there were four each night) shouted "halt who goes there and wanted the password". The password changed every day and neither Sarge nor I knew it. Finally, Sarge said, and I quote "Dammit, don't fucking shoot, this is Sarge and we're coming in". Funny as hell.

One time, my buddy "Joe Sampson" and I had to make a run to Division Headquarters and on the way, we passed through several villages. It was winter and very cold, and a bunch of locals were throwing snowballs at my Jeep. We happened to have a big bucket in the Jeep and "Joe" filled it with cold water and said, on the way back, stop, and he would throw it on them. I stopped and he soaked them. Thank God, I was able to get going or they would have killed us.

People were in really dire straits at the time and would steal anything that wasn't nailed down. When I went to Seoul or Inchon on business, I always took a chain and a padlock and locked my vehicle to a telephone pole or something.

We had another little episode worth mentioning. Our "CO" received a request to send a couple of squads to another unit's area for a week or so. They were going on Maneuvers and needed someone to provide security for their Camp while they were gone. With little to do, Me and a couple of buddies decided to check out some shot guns from the Armory and go pheasant hunting. Unbeknownst to us, we were hunting in a mine field. A lieutenant showed up and saw us from the top of a hill. He told us to come up there and he took our names and reported us to our commanding officer. We did kill a pheasant though and the cook fixed it for us. We also found some "Asahi" beer to go along with it (that our Hosts had left behind). Our commanding officer ordered us to pull some extra duty when we got back to our unit.

Annyeong Korea, haeng-un-eul-bibnida, (goodbye Korea and good luck).

Korean war memorial in Washington, DC.

There are 19 statues representing the Army, Navy, Marines and Air Force. The troops are walking thru a field of scrubby bushes and wear ponchos covering their weapons and equipment which seem to be blowing in the cold Korean wind.

Chapter 7: The First Marine Division comes home (Mar. 1955).

After 5 years in Korea, the 1st Marine Division was finally brought home. We arrived in San Diego on March 18, 1955. We disembarked and assembled in the San Diego baseball stadium. There were speeches by politicians, celebrities, etc. and then we had a big parade, up the main street leading to Balboa Park. Once there, we were loaded on buses and taken to Camp Pendleton. Camp Pendleton consists of 125,000 acres and is Approx. 48 miles north of San Diego and 92 miles south of Los Angeles.

Our company was housed in an area, that I believe was called Area 33. Concrete barracks, mess hall, motor pool, supply depot, etc. The first Marine division had brought back 5,500 men from Korea, so naturally we weren't all housed in the same area. Camp Pendleton is the headquarters of the 1st Marine Division.

We soon settled into a typical Marine Corp's routine. Formation in the morning, calisthenics, chow, close order drill, hiking, a class occasionally, cleaning our barracks and weapons, inspections, maintaining our vehicles, etc. We would also go on "maneuvers" or have what they called "a firing problem" periodically.

A firing problem simply meant we would load some of our mortars on trailers and along with the members of our mortar platoons, go to the firing range and fire a number of practice rounds into the impact area (which was littered with old trucks, tanks, etc.). You were firing over the top of a hill, so you could not see your target. A mortar is aimed by the combination of elevation, angle to the ground-horizontal, and azimuth, the traverse adjustment-side to side. It's all much simpler now with GPS. The way a 4.2 mortar works is relatively simple. The mortar man drops the shell down the tube, the shell hits a fixed firing pin, which ignites the propellant charges and the gas created pushes the shell out of the tube. We had an observation post on top of the hill that we were firing over, so the forward observation man could observe where the shells were landing and radio back adjustments. I was up there several times with our "CO" and wasn't particularly fond of those shells going over our head.

Since I was the only driver in our Company that had an "explosives license", I could not get a leave. I had one 21 day leave in two years. I had to come up with a plan. I called mom in Tennessee (They had just gotten home from Spain and had not left yet for dad's first stint in Ecuador) and I told her to call the "Red Cross" and tell them my Granny was very ill and I wanted to see her before she died. The "Red Cross" then got in touch with my "CO" and I flew home on a 21 day leave in October of 1955.

Subsequently, I bought a 1951 Ford and drove it back from LaFollette, Tennessee to Camp Pendleton, California (mostly on the legendary route 66).

We normally got weekend passes three times a month and the guys would fan out around the area. One weekend I was in Hollywood with a friend "Joe Samson" (Cajun), and we decided to check out the girls at the "Hollywood Palladium" on Sunset Blvd. It was a nightclub with a huge dancefloor and live Orchestra. The only problem was that you had to have on a jacket and necktie to get in. So, as you will notice in the attached photo, we both had to buy the same jacket and neckties. We look like the Bobbsey Twins (ha). The Palladium has been in business for 82 years and the opening act on Sept. 23, 1940, was "The Tommy Dorsey Orchestra" featuring the soon to be famous "Frank Sinatra".

Me (on the left) and Joe Samson at the Palladium, March 20, 1955.

Another little episode was when I got locked up for 5 days in the Santa Anna jail. One Friday evening I had a date with a waitress at the Greyhound bus station in Los Angeles. I was running a little late and was going too fast thru Santa Anna and got a ticket. I was ordered to report to court on Monday morning and the judge said he was tired of Marines speeding through his town and sentenced me to 5 days in the Santa Anna jail. Since I only had one day off, to go to court, that made me 4 days "AWOL" when I got back to Pendleton on Friday. I then had what they called "Colonel's office hours" and he said since I drove my car that fast, he didn't want me driving Marine Corps vehicles. I was taken out of the motor pool and put in supply. What the Colonel didn't know, I was the only person in our company with an "explosives license" and so the very next time we went on maneuvers, they had to take me out of supply and put me back in the motor pool, so I could haul that dangerous ordinance. PS: I never saw that cute little waitress again.

We did make one amphibious landing at the beach near Oceanside. I don't remember the number of units (troops) involved, but I do remember this operation being a little bit tricky. "LST'S" were used for this assault, and they got as close to the beach as possible, lowered their ramps and then we, the truck drivers (with troops and equipment on board) had to drive down onto floating, overlapping platforms to make it to the beach. The only problem with this little scenario was that you had to dart from one platform to the next when they were at the same level in the water. Some years later, they were attempting the same type of landing, at the same location, and one of the trucks (full of troops) got its wheels off on one side of a platform, turned upside down and sank in the ocean. A number of young Marines drowned.

Amphibious landings can be dangerous. Nine Marines were killed on July 30th, 2020, when an "AAV" (amphibious assault vehicle) started leaking and sank near San Clemente Island. The "AAV" being used in this most recent accident was 35 years old and in poor condition.

We had a similar situation in Korea with our vehicles, no spare parts, gas with water in it. We had to lay down in the damn dirt and take the plugs out of our gas tanks and drain the water out about once a month, so they would run halfway decent.

There's a couple more little incidents at Camp Pendleton that stand out in my memory. Camp Pendleton is huge (125,000 acres). We went on "maneuvers" one time and were in the field for about 3 days. The Marine Corp's always insists on everything being as realistic as possible, so they even had us set up a field kitchen in a twelve-man squad tent. One evening our cook, "Chambers", the guy from New Jersey, "Joisy", had to cook fresh Burgers from ground beef that had been delivered to our camp site. The field stoves were fueled by propane and the fresh ground beef was sitting on a table in big pans (the tent was not ventilated). Lo and behold the fumes from the propane stoves settled in the meat and when we sat down to eat everything tasted like propane. Chambers was not only embarrassed, but mad as hell, especially when we started harassing him about it. They gave us some "C-Rations" for supper.

Another time the "Mortar Platoons" were on some sort of a "field Problem" and our "CO" wanted me to take him out in a Jeep to see how things were going. Well Camp Pendleton is extremely large and some places rough as hell. Using maps and a two-way radio, we finally located them. The captain did his little inspection and then we headed back to "Area 33". I remember going around the side of a hill and our jeep was so close to turning over that the captain was holding on to sage grass to help keep us upright. Like that would really help (ha). I am not bragging, but he said I was the best jeep driver he had ever had, in all his years in the Marine Corp's. I guess he appreciated the fact that I didn't turn over and kill him.

I hope, with all the money that's been appropriated in the last several years, that our troops (in all branches of the service) have equipment in good working order. Their lives depend on it.

I was discharged on Sept. 14th, 1956, and headed home to LaFollette in my "51 Ford". It was an extremely rough trip. Overheating in Arizona (it had been 117 degrees that day), then I ran out of gas, but luckily someone stopped and gave me a ride to the next town (I got a can of gas and hired a taxi to take me back to my car), Blowing oil (I had to stop and add a quart about every 100 miles), then my generator gave out and by the time I limped into LaFollette, my head lights were putting out about as much light as two Lightning bugs.

Note: This is the 1956 Ford Fairlane that my dad gave me when I got out of the Marine Corps. It was waiting for me when I got home from California. I loved that car.

Chapter 8: Discharged and back home in Tenn. (1956-1957).

Mom was still there when I got to Granny's, but dad had already left for his first, two-year stint in Ecuador. My "51 Ford" was shot, but dad had left me a brand new "1956 Ford" (see photo above) sitting in front of my Granny's house. It was red and black, with white sidewall tires and I added dual antennas on the rear fenders. My mom stayed for several more weeks and then joined dad in Ecuador.

I enrolled immediately in Fulton Vocational training center in Knoxville on the G.I. bill and took mechanical drafting and design. We had a certain amount of work to get done in one year and part of that was learning how to sketch. Sometimes the Prof. would allow us to leave the classroom and go outside to sketch. There was a pool room several blocks away and I think we sketched a lot of Pool balls. I finished all my requirements in about 10-1/2 months.

I came home from school one evening and parked in front of my Granny's house and someone knocked on the door. I opened the door and Tennessee highway patrolman "Green" grabbed me by the belt and told me to get in the patrol car. What had happened, two guys had run him off the road several miles north of my Granny's and since they had a car the same color as mine, He assumed it was me. There was a rental property across the road from my Granny and the lady who lived there was the county's most famous prostitute (Big Red). When Green started to pull out, she hollered at him and said that I was not the one that ran him off the road. Those "ass holes" had paid her a little visit on their way down the road and told her about their incident with Officer Green. She saved my butt, thank you "Big Red". Oh-by the way, I went by officer green's house about a week later and asked him if he got those two guys that ran him off the road and he said yes but did not offer me an apology.

I met my future wife "Roberta" in LaFollette, probably in October 1956. She was a junior at "Wynn High school" and lived with her mom and Dad, about nine miles north of LaFollette. She played basketball, was a member of the "Beta club" and had been an evangelical Christian practically all her life and started attending church at a young age, so I had to mind my manners when we went out.

I guess you would say we had an on again, off again romance (never went steady) until we were married the following July 1st, 1957. The evening I asked her to marry me was kind of strange. She and I and her first cousin "Elnoria" had been for a ride down to "Norris Dam" and had just come back and parked in a parking lot next to a church in LaFollette. I got down on one knee, took her by the hand and asked her to marry me. She said yes. I must have been excited, because I went right up the street, ran a stop sign and broad sided a taxi. Thankfully, no one was injured. The reason I wanted to get married, on kind of short notice, was because I was coming to Cincinnati to look for a job as soon as I finished school and didn't want to lose her. She was, in my opinion, so pretty and such a good person.

Roberta Leigh (Walden) Davis

Richard J. Davis Jr.

THE DAY ROBERTA AND I GOT MARRIED (JULY 1ST, 1957)

We made plans to elope, and I swore "Elnoria" to secrecy because I knew that Roberta's mom and dad would not agree for her to marry with another year left in high school. We took another cousin with us as a witness (required at the time if either person was under 18, Roberta was seventeen and a half) and we were married by a "justice of the peace" in Clinton, Tennessee. When we came back and told her mom "Sarah" that we were married, she about fainted. I appeased her somewhat by telling her that Roberta could stay in Tennessee for an additional year and finish high school. I then told my new wife "Let's get out of here" and we went to Gatlinburg on a short honeymoon.

Well, "Sarah", you can rest in peace, our union brought forth three fine sons, ten Grandchildren, and so far, seven Great Grandchildren with Davis and Walden blood running through their veins. In my opinion, there is no greater legacy than that.

Roberta Leigh, Sarah Eller (their mom) and Geraldine Ann Walden. Early 1950s.

Chapter 9: Coming to Cincinnati and raising a family (1957-).

I came to Cincinnati shortly after getting out of vocational college to look for a job. I was hired the first week by a Company, at that time, called "Cincinnati Milling Machine and Grinders Inc.", later changed to "Cincinnati Milacron". I subsequently worked there for forty years (1957 to 1997) and went back for nine more years as a sub-contractor. At the time I started, they were the largest machine tool builder in the world with approx. 15,000 employees. I did design and drafting in the Electrical Engineering Dept. on a drawing board for about 20 years and then (in 1977), myself and a co-worker received computer training at "Dec" Corporation in Wooster, Mass. and helped write the specifications for the software (coding) to be done by "Dec" that was required to set up the "electrical engineering application" back at "Milacron". Once the application was firm, we brought other people on board and started making electrical drawings on the computer (CAD-computer aided design) and our production gains were amazing. Mechanical and Hydraulic engineering followed soon thereafter. They mostly used "CAD" software that was already commercially available.

My wife finished high school in May of 1958 and came to Cincinnati. We rented for six years and bought a house in 1963 (east side of Cincinnati) and set about raising our three sons. They were born in 1959, 1961, and 1968. We had the usual trials and tribulations that most young families encounter, but I think everyone who has ever raised a family pretty much knows that drill, so I am not going to bore you with the mundane.

I will though tell you some stories about things that have happened over the last sixty-five years. Some funny, some interesting, some different.

We had a large lot (60 ft. x 943 ft.), so we kind of had some options as to what we could do. We eventually had three areas fenced in behind our house, each one about sixty feet square and ended up with a menagerie. I built a chicken house, so we had chickens, four ponies at different times, a dog, a cat, rabbits, ducks. I'm sure the neighbors thought we were a bunch of Hillbilly's, but they were wrong. We just wanted our boys to be exposed to different animals and always kept our place neat and clean. We were heavily involved in Soccer for nine or ten years and I coached for 3 years. I worked with several Germans at "Milacron" and they, along with others, were instrumental in forming a soccer league. It was called

"Say" Soccer (soccer association youth) and gave many kids an opportunity to play. Soccer is currently becoming much more popular in America.

The boys also worked part time jobs while in High school. The oldest Caddied, worked at a farm store. I think about the first day they gave him a shot gun and had him killing groundhogs in their corn fields. He also worked at a nursery and craft shop.

The next oldest worked at two of the same three places. I remember one time it was blue cold, and they had him outside selling Christmas trees. My wife and I took him some hot chocolate to warm him up. Next came the younger brother. He worked at a buffet and was a machinist co-op apprentice in his senior year.

Our three fine sons. L TO R: Brian, Mike, Rick

Our little girl Monique

My wife Roberta was a good cook and housekeeper and although we didn't have any money to spare, we always tried to keep our boys well fed. We ate a lot of fried potatoes, green beans, pinto beans, corn bread, spaghetti, soup, etc. I would make pancakes sometimes on Sunday mornings and thought I was never going to get through. Those big boys could sure put them away. Roberta always made them go to church on Sunday morning's and didn't allow any drinking, smoking or foul language in the house. We tried to lay a foundation. Now I'm not saying everything was perfect, it was not, but I do think we did a pretty good job.

All three boys finished high school, have a good work ethic and have been gainfully employed since they were old enough to enter the workforce, obtaining additional education and/or training along the way to make them all very proficient at their jobs. They collectively have ten children between them and seven Grandchildren, so the Davis/Walden family tree has lots of foliage.

What my Mom and Dad were doing in the 50's and early 60's:

A couple of other funny things happened along the way. As I mentioned earlier, Mom and Dad came home from Spain in 1955. They had been there while I was in Korea. Dad was working on a Radar installation being built near Zaragoza. Every time Dad did an overseas job, he would always send Mom home early and then he would have movers come in and pack everything that they wanted to ship back to the states and shut down the house. Mom figured dad would fly to New York (which she had done) and take a Greyhound bus or train to Tennessee. Well, when the time came that he was supposed to be home, he didn't show up. So, she called the Airlines and cruise ship company and found out that he had taken a Mediterranean cruise and came across the Atlantic to New York by ship. She was so aggravated that she went to New York and met the ship at the dock and gave him an in-person ass chewing when he came down the ramp.

Dad then took a job in Ecuador and went down there in late 1956. Mom joined him not long after I got home from the Marines. He worked there for four years (doing highway engineering) and one of the things that made me proud was his inflexibility when it came to doing his job. The "specs" called for a pond to be graded next to a village that the highway passed by (to give the people a water supply) and the construction company wanted to skip it and dad told them, "Hell no", the specs called for it and they were going to grade that pond.

The next job dad took was two years doing highway engineering in Liberia. He designed the first "Clover Leaf" in that country. A couple of funny little instances, dad had a trailer and when they were out in the "Bush", he would sometimes stay there and not come home to "Monrovia" for several days. Well one night the Chief of one of the tribes came to dad's trailer and offered him a young female companion for the night. I don't remember him ever telling me whether he took the Chief up on his offer.

A funny thing that happened with my mom. There was a large building back behind where mom and dad lived in "Monrovia" and mom said about twenty people lived in it. One day mom looked out her kitchen window and one of their "male" neighbors was laying in her back yard "naked" sunbathing. I'm not going to repeat it, but what she said to him was "R-rated" and put him on the run.

Another little episode that occurred in the late 50's. "Michael Baker International" contacted Dad. They were doing the civil engineering on the new "Turfway Park" being built in northern Kentucky and their Engineer had either quit or been fired and they asked Dad to come up from Tennessee and finish the job, which he did. He laid out the track for them, the access roads, location for the stables, etc. I never gave it much thought, but he told me that he located the stables downwind from the grandstand, so the race fans didn't have to smell horse manure while watching the races. Once, while he was up here, we went down to Tennessee one weekend to visit mom and drove Dad's Ford. When we came back on Sunday evening, we had a big red rooster in a cardboard box that my wife's dad Theodore Walden had given us (we had chickens at our home in Cincinnati at the time). Well, as luck would have it, that Ford overheated about five miles or so from home and we had to call a cab. Me, my wife, my dad, and that rooster had to pile in that cab to finish our trip. I bet that cab. Driver thought, what a bunch of hillbillies. (Ha)

Since Roberta's parents, my Granny and other family members lived in Tennessee, we went down to visit as often as possible. We happened to go down in early 1961 and I wanted to go by and say hello to my uncle "John" and his family. We stopped by and I remember the last thing he said was "come back down in late April and we'll gig some frogs". I never saw him alive again as he was run over by a "hit and run" driver and killed shortly thereafter. I went back to Tennessee for his funeral, but my wife couldn't go because she was pregnant with our second son and did not feel like making the trip. John was forty-five years old at the time and had 7 children.

Every time I used to hear the "Jimmy Dean" song "big john", I would always think of my uncle John, especially the last line "at the bottom of this mine lies one hell of a man, "big john". Tragic, I sure missed him.

John and his Wife Edna's youngest Son "William Long" that we always referred to as "Little Bill" was killed in Vietnam several years later. He was eighteen years old and had just gotten married before he went to Nam. His name is on "The Vietnam Memorial Wall" in Washington. R.I.P. young man.

William (Little Bill) Long, My First Cousin.

John and Edna's oldest son "John Earl Long," was a very good Basketball player at LaFollette high school and had a great one-hand jump shot. In 1958 he got a scholarship to a junior college in Mississippi, "Perkinston junior college" and then an additional two-year scholarship to "Delta State university". Eventually getting his masters and PHD from "Southern Mississippi University". In 1960 he was the state record holder in the one-mile run and had top three finishes in the long jump and the 800-yard run. He then embarked on a 40-year teaching and coaching career and was eventually school superintendent. We are all proud of him. He worked hard, applied himself and made it out of the "Poverty Pocket", which is what my mom used to call Campbell County, Tennessee.

John Earl Long (Delta State University), My First Cousin.

My wife's parents "Theodore and Sarah" lived about nine miles north of LaFollette and were just good old country folks. Theodore worked some in the coal mines in his younger days, but eventually became a carpenter and worked in Tennessee and other places like Baltimore, Cincinnati, Oak Ridge, etc. Sarah, worked as a cook at "Wynn" school for many years and cooked her two Daughters (my wife Roberta and her sister Geraldine) thru high school. Theodore had four brothers and Sarah had one sister and four brothers.

My wife used to talk about how the "Walden boys" would come out of "Walden Hollow" on Sundays to go courting. Each boy wore a white shirt, which had just been ironed by their mother. Since they had no electricity, she had to iron their shirts with a "flat iron", heated on the wood burning cook stove. Theodore and His brother Earnest would cut across the mountain to "Hickory creek" because they were courting sisters (Sarah and Mary Reynolds, who lived there).

They made a nice garden each year and Sarah did a lot of canning and freezing of produce, plus making apple and blackberry jelly, etc. Of course, like most country folks, they had a chicken house with a few chickens and sometimes a hog to kill in the fall. I think Theodore knew where every apple tree or blackberry bush was in Campbell County, so it was rare for him to come home and not have something for Sarah to either cook or can. I remember one time he came home with some pumpkins and my wife happened to be in Tennessee at the time and Sarah loaded one of the pumpkins into her car and as they went toward town, she said, "pull over here" and she got out and threw the pumpkin down over the hill and then said and I quote "that's one pumpkin Theodore Walden is not going to get".

Theodore was a kind of unique person. On one hand he was inquisitive and somewhat innovative and on the other hand he had this wry sense of humor. He handed me a pistol once and said quote "let's see you hit that nail head in the door of the outhouse". Well, I don't profess to be a good pistol shot, but I took careful aim and drilled it and he didn't quite know what to say.

I heard another story recently about Theodore. It seems that my wife's cousin "LB" went down to his house one time and Theodore had a stack of paint cans on the porch of the smoke house and He was shooting at them with his pistol. Every time a bullet hit a can, it flew up in the air and slung paint all over. He evidently thought that was funny. I think this was in the days before he got religion and I figure he might have been sipping on a little "Tennessee shine" that day.

One time he had my youngest son roll a tire up a big hill (which is a tough job) and when they got to the top, my son asked, "what do you want me to do now Papaw" and he replied, "now turn it loose and let's see it roll back down the hill".

Another comical thing, he made a harness once for two geese and had them on a leash going back and forth picking the bugs off his beans and strawberries.

He also built a little "motor driven trolley" that would bring firewood down off the mountain behind his house, dump it and return empty. It sure saved a lot of walking.

When we happened to be in Tennessee, we would often eat breakfast at Theodore and Sarah's house, and he would always take me to the basement before breakfast to do what he called "cut the cob-webs out of our throats". What that meant was taking a swig of "shine" before breakfast. Man, that "Tennessee shine" will burn the hair off your tongue.

My wife used to tell a little story about her "Granny Julia" (Sarah's mother) who lived with Theodore and Sarah. Television was in its infancy when She and Her Sister Geraldine were growing up and Granny Julia liked to watch "Tenn. Ernie Ford". Well Granny didn't quite understand the concept and She thought "Tenn. Ernie" could also see them. Roberta said, just for fun, She and Gerry would pull their skirts up slightly and Granny would always say, and I quote "you girls are just going to make plumb nothings".

A story I was told was about Theodore's father "John Frank". He and his wife "Luerany" were living in a little house up in Walden Hollow. One night when John Frank went to bed, there was a snake inside the "straw tick" that he was sleeping on. When he would roll over, he could also feel the snake moving around. I was told that he didn't get up during the night, but I would assume he got rid of that damn snake the next morning.

A couple of funny little Cincinnati stories. Theodore was staying at my wife's sister's apartment one time and needed to use the bathroom, so he went down to the garage (where there was a bathroom) and was doing his thing and the landlady happened to open the door (she didn't know he was in there). I said, what did you do? He said, I just looked up and said "Howdy". She was old and just about fainted.

Theodore was at our house one time doing some remodeling in the basement. He mashed his finger with the hammer, and I asked the boys what he had to say. They said he walked over, opened the window, and shouted "shit" out the window, as loud as he could. He didn't curse much, but this was one time he just had to cut loose.

My mother-in-law "Sarah" was a hard worker, excellent cook and baker and could put a great meal on the table Faster than anyone I ever saw. Something like Fried chicken, chopped steak and gravy, fried taters, green beans, cream corn, cold slaw, fresh maters, green onions, corn bread, sweet tea and maybe a good blackberry cobbler or Italian cream cake. She also used to make stack cakes and jam cakes around Christmas time. Yum, Yum, gotta get you some.

My Dad retired in the early 1960's, and he and my mom lived with Granny Long in LaFollette. They would come to Cincinnati to visit occasionally, and we would go down to Tennessee from time to time.

I remember the day "Elvis Presley" passed away. My wife and I were always Elvis fans, because, when we were dating in late 1956, and early 1957, He was releasing a new song about every week. Well, he just happened to pass away on August 16th, 1977, which was our youngest sons' ninth birthday. I remember him coming out of his bedroom and being upset because my wife and I were mourning Elvis' death and weren't paying much attention to his birthday. We got to see Elvis in person several years before he passed, and I remember him introducing a new song called "Hurt" and the crowd liking it so much, he sang it twice. Great singer, great concert.

My Mom took a trip to the "Holy Land" with her sister Rhoda in 1978. Rhoda kept a diary of their trip and wrote a very good fifteen-page description of it when they got back.

Sarah used to tell a story about one time she rode to Cincinnati with my mom and dad. We were still living in an apartment at the time and there was a road near us called "Duck Creek". Well, they went back and forth on 'Duck Creek" for God knows how long, trying to find our house. It was cold weather, and Sarah was in the back seat with a box of frozen food between her feet. She said, my dad got frustrated, jerked his teeth out of his mouth, put them in his pocket, lit up a cigarette and rolled his window down. She said she just about froze. (ha)

My Granny passed away in 1971, at the age of 89 and my mom passed away in 1981, at the age of 69. Mom died of a cancerous tumor next to her lung. She was always a heavy smoker, and, in my opinion, this surely contributed to her relatively young death.

Dad continued to live in LaFollette by himself from the time mom passed away until December of 1991. My wife and me and the boys would kind of alternate going down to see him. He always liked for us to bring him a bottle of Rum and some little "Erik cigars". We went down to see him at Christmas 1991, and he was sick with the flu, and I insisted that he come back to Cincinnati with us. He lived with my wife and me for approx. one year and then started having some serious kidney problems and the doctor suggested we put him in a nursing home. He was in the nursing home for about six months and passed away on Friday, May 21st, 1993, one day shy of his 99th birthday. I had ordered a cake and we were going to have a little party for him the next day at the nursing home. He was rarely sick during his lifetime and evidently had very good genes.

Some deer hunting stories before we bought the farm:

I think this might be a good place to start telling some interesting stories about when me and the boys got into deer hunting. The two older boys had been hunting for several years when the youngest decided He wanted to start. He was fourteen at the time and my wife thought it might be wise for me to start hunting also, because of his age. We subsequently pretty much hunted on publicly available land in Kentucky for about the next eight years. Fort Knox, Land between the lakes, Lloyd's WMA, etc. Some of these public hunting places are like being in combat, especially on opening day. I remember the first opening day at Lloyd's, there was so damn much shooting that you could hear the shells whizzing through the trees, so I hit the deck until it calmed down a little bit.

I remember one funny little episode at Lloyds. I was hunting with a Marlin, 30-30 lever action rifle and was kind of hid behind a tree. A Buck came down out of the woods across from me and I got a little excited and missed my first shot. The deer didn't know where the shot came from and ran straight at me, I fired probably five more times (from the hip). He then veered off to my left and ran maybe 100 feet and stopped and looked back at me. I then took careful aim and pulled the trigger and "click", I was out of ammo. After that the boys called me "The Rifleman" (a-la Chuck Conners) for a long time. They then insisted I get rid of the Marlin and switch to a Remington Model 700, 30-06 bolt action rifle with a scope.

Another little story about hunting at "Lloyds". My oldest and middle son were Bow hunting there one time and they were up in trees on each side of a field and could see each other. After a while, my oldest son said he saw his brother fall out of his tree and hit the ground, thump. Well, his bow was still up in the tree, so he started to climb back up and when he took ahold of a limb, it broke and he fell again, thump. What had happened, he had fallen asleep when he fell out of the tree the first time.

We had another funny thing happen on a hunting trip to "Fort Knox". The way it works is, you apply and if you are picked, you are assigned a guide. We drove down on Friday evening, stayed at a motel, and met our guide in a designated parking lot early on Saturday morning. The guide gives a talk about the rules and regulations before leading his little convoy onto the base. Well one of the things not allowed is alcohol. You cannot bring booze onto the base, period. We had forgotten to leave our cooler at the motel and didn't have time to go back. We happened to be in a parking lot, of like, a closed K-Mart and there were three semis parked next to it. One of the guys said, let's just set the cooler inside the rear tire of one of the trucks and pick it up when we come out this evening. Well, when we came out in the evening, all three trucks were gone and so was our cooler. Some trucker probably said "Cha-Ching" baby.

This is me with two eight pointers and a ten pointer that I killed. The ten pointer was killed at "Fort Knox" (with a twelve-gage slug) on Dec. 10th, 1989, in sub-zero temperatures. The two eight pointers were killed at our farm in Owen County KY.

Chapter 10: **Triple D Farm and "The Colonel".**

Me and two of my sons eventually bought a farm in northern Kentucky (in 1990) and have had a good place to hunt for Over thirty years. They also do quite a bit of fishing, mostly at Lake Cumberland and Laken Erie. Several of the grand kids have been into hunting and fishing for some time now.

We have had a good run at the farm. My youngest son lived for years in the original farmhouse and my middle son and I both built cabins. We planted a bunch of pine trees, bought, and raised some cattle, had several horses, built a bunch of tree stands, etc. and used to have a thing each year that we called "farm fest", which was basically getting together for a good meal, hayrides, etc. Sometimes we would have close to a hundred people show up. One year we roasted a pig and I remember taking turns sitting up all night with that "son of a gun". We only did that once.

A funny story about the farm that wasn't funny at the time. We did not have any ATV'S (four wheeler's) until several years after we bought the farm. If someone killed a deer, we would just drag it up to flat ground and then haul it to the house or one of the cabins with a Pickup truck. One cold November morning, I was walking to the back of the farm to a tree stand and had to cross the creek on a big sycamore tree that had fallen across it. Well, I got about halfway across and fell in, and my rifle and glasses went to the bottom of the creek. The water level was about waist high, and I had to go underwater to try and retrieve them. I was lucky and found them both, but that's not the end of the story. I then had to walk all the way back to my cabin soaking wet. I about froze, but survived, and still laugh every time I remember that little episode.

Another thing we have been doing for years is getting together on the night before opening day of modern gun season for what we call "wild game dinner". Basically, the idea is that all the meat eaten has pretty much been killed or caught by someone in the family. Deer meat, wild turkey, fish (usually caught at Lake Erie or Lake Cumberland), etc.

After my dad passed away, we all went to Tennessee for his funeral and my first cousin (Col. Raymond L. "buddy" Norman) came up from Florida. My boys said to me after the funeral, why don't you invite "Buddy" to come up and hunt with us, he accepted and subsequently came up to hunt for about the next 20 years.

A little history about "The Colonel":

Colonel Raymond L. "Buddy" Norman, USAF

Buddy spent most of his entire career in the military. He was in the paratroopers for five years and then in the Air Force for twenty-nine years, achieving the rank of Colonel. A distinguished Flying Cross recipient, he was the first fighter Pilot to complete one hundred missions over North Vietnam. Buddy ran away to join the military many times, starting at age 15, always fibbing about his age. Finally at age 16 his Mother Rhoda Ann said, "we might as well let him go". He went thru basic training and was shipped to Germany in 1945, right at the end of the war.

Buddy's Air Force career was like watching the movie "The Right Stuff". As a matter of fact, Bud knew many legends such as Chuck Yeager and Neil Armstrong. He flew everything from P51 Mustangs to "hot rod" F4 Phantoms on aerial reconnaissance over North Vietnam. Buddy said his plane was much faster due to no armaments, just cameras. He told of how he knew about 50% of the POW pilots when they were released after the war.

As a sidenote just to settle this once and for all. According to Bud, when "Jane Fonda" visited Vietnam, they had to suspend bombing missions to avoid the PR nightmare of accidently killing 'Hanoi Jane". The North Vietnamese took full advantage of this "cease fire" to rebuild their ground defenses. This treachery cost American lives. In my opinion, she should have been tried for treason.

Hanoi Jane

An entire book could be written about Buddy. He once told us of his involvement in the recovery of the World War II USAAF B-24D Liberator. The remains of the plane were discovered in November 1958, by a British Oil exploration team in the Libyan desert over 15 years after their disappearance. Apparently, they became lost in a sandstorm after a bombing run and were forced to land in the desert. Buddy was involved in the recovery of our soldiers remains. He told of flying missions with sophisticated sonar and that they located all but one of our boys. He took a lot of pride in bringing them home.

Another interesting story Bud told was about the snakes in that area of the world. You see, most land based aerial missions during the Vietnam war were flown out of Thailand. He said that due to the rainy season the Air Force built elevated runways. These served as the perfect spot for all sorts of creatures to get out of the water. Bud said one time he was being taken to his F4 Phantom in a jeep and they saw a King Cobra on the runway. For those of you that don't know, a King Cobra is a feared and revered animal in India and Southeast Asia. These awesome and deadly creatures can grow up the 19 feet long! They can stand up 1/3 of their length. They made the decision the snake would have to be killed for the safety of the air crews. Bud told the driver to radio the tower and let them know they were not under attack. Bud dispatched the snake with an M16 they had in the Jeep. He said he tried to shoot it with his sidearm, but it would not hold still long enough.

Buddy's Paratrooper platoon marching up Gay St., Knoxville, TN. c.1947

As you can probably tell by now, Buddy was quite a storyteller. A favorite pass time when we would get together at deer camp was to listen to his exploits. He was not a braggard mind you. He just loved our country and the military. He once told of being involved with testing of air to air, "Nuclear weapons" during the cold war. The idea was you could fire a nuke into a group of airplanes and destroy them all at once. Bud said he got pulled off the mission to go to Europe for some classified work that required his level of security clearance. He was asked to recommend a pilot to take his place which he did. Part of this mission included detonating one of these devices in midair, then flying back thru the radiation cloud to gather data in a specially shielded airplane (so they thought). His replacement did his job and collected the data. Unfortunately, he was dead within one year of cancer. Although Bud had not known it was unsafe, it turned out the precautions were not sufficient. Bud said to that day he felt bad recommending this other pilot.

He always brought us some homemade strawberry wine when he came up. You see these commercials about the "most interesting man in the world" and it should have been Buddy sitting there. Buddy could sit around the campfire and point out every major star and constellation in the sky.

All I can say was he was a hell of a good man, a good shot with a rifle and our family hero and a true Patriot. Rest in peace Colonel.

L to R: Mike, Brian, Roberta, Me, and Rick at the farm.

L to R: Mike, Me, Rick, Brian and "The Colonel" at the farm. Look at those big boys, I have a pretty good security detail there.

My wife Roberta on "Dusty Go-Boy" and Mike on "Spider".

THE NEW FARM (A POEM WRITTEN BY MY 96-YEAR-OLD DAD).

The New Farm

They bought a farm named it 3 D's
They cleared and grubbed, They planted trees.
They built a house and porch with a view.
They laughed and built an "outhouse" new
They scraped and painted, joked a lot.
Hopefully planted a garden spot.
They built for the present, the future in mind
strived to make the best of it's kind.
They shared their hopes and dreams and pride.
You just can't match that Davis Stride.

Roberta sighed "there's so much to be done"
Beth replied "it's going to be fun"
Michael grumbled "I have too much land".
Ricky answered "I'll give you a hand".
Nancy chirped "and what about me".
Brian suggested "go plant a tree".
Richard announced "I have planning to do"
and ambled off to outhouse new.
Outhouse new, the work of man
A place to sit and dream and plan.

The Entrance Sign among the best,
it greets the folks, welcomes the guest's
It appears to glow, when company arrives.
Another example of the Davis Stride.

The deer are here, they come and go,
'Bout time for Mike to shoot a doe.

The main house old, looks good as new
New windows added improve the view.
Most important addition I'll say,
A new family member has come to stay.

Pop Davis 10-15-90

Chapter 11: **The South and it's People (Yesterday, Today and Forever).**

I am not a Psychiatrist and probably should not be giving my opinion on how southern people think, how they feel and what their general outlook on life is, but after listening to some of these arrogant television Anchors, Politicians and talking heads on TV for years, criticizing southern people and giving their opinions on about every subject, and about half the time, not knowing what the hell their talking about, I feel liberated.

It is difficult to define a "southern person" these day's since we are such a homogenized society. I guess a "southern person" is a person who was primarily born and raised in the south and understands the traditions and language.

You can't make an observation without there being some exceptions, but southern people (both men and women) were hard workers, they had to be to survive. My focus though is primarily on country folks in Southern Appalachia. As we often say, "back in the old days", a lot of the men either worked in the coal mines or logging woods, some were farmers, some did both, etc., and there was also a large contingent (mostly during and after World War two) who worked in places like Oak Ridge or came north to places like Cincinnati, Baltimore, Detroit, Dayton, Indianapolis, etc. to look for work. If possible, they tried to go home on the weekends.

Everyone had a garden, maybe a hog and a few chickens and both the men and women shared a lot of the hard outside work, but the men (generally speaking), did not cook or do housework. A women's work was pretty much never done unless she was just plumb "no account" (a southern term). Prior to getting electricity, they heated their houses with a wood/coal stove or fireplace, cooked on a wood burning cook stove, heated their water and irons on the stove, washed clothes on a wash board in a galvanized tub, rung them out and hung them on a line outside to dry, they sometimes boiled extra dirty clothes outside in one of those big black iron kettles, canned all kinds of fruits and vegetables, and were expected to put three squares (meals) on the table each day.

Houses, for the most part, were lit by Kerosene lamps and since there was little to do after dark, many people went to bed early, got up early, and some had extremely large families. I think there is a connection to be made there. One of my wife's uncles was responsible for fourteen children. I knew many other families with eight, ten, or twelve children. My own Granny had eight.

Sunday was generally a day of rest for the men, but the women were still expected to put three squares (meals) on the board (table). Churches were the focal point of most rural communities and if you were a member, and what some churches call "Saved" and "A born again Christian", you were pretty much expected to be there every time the door was opened, period. If you didn't go, the Pastor might come calling.

The Pastor is almost always invited to some one's house for lunch (dinner) after church. In case you are wondering, a lot of southern people call the noon meal "dinner" and the evening meal "supper". My "mother-in-law" often had the Pastor to her house for "dinner" after church and she usually had fried chicken and chopped steak with gravy and of course all the fixings. Now, not everyone went to church on a regular basis, but they all showed up for the "homecoming" or as it was called "dinner on the ground", because there was lots of food. Many young men waited outside to walk the young lass's home after church.

A typical little country church with a cemetery next to it.

If there was to be a "baptizing" take place on a particular Sunday, it was usually done in a nearby creek or pond. In many southern churches, the women almost always wore dresses to church (one of the other ladies would pin the hem of their dress together before they went into the water), and they, along with the Pastor would wade right out into the water and he would say something like "Because you've professed your faith in the Lord Jesus, I now baptize you in the name of the Father, The Son and The Holy ghost, Amen". He would then lower them into the water, submerge them completely and then raise them back up.

The photo below is of a typical 'Church of God" baptizing taking place under a bridge (the white bridge) on US25W, approx. 10 miles north of LaFollette, Tennessee. Included in the photo are my wife's mother "Sarah Walden", her uncle 'Mitt Walden", Another uncle "Dink Reynolds and his wife Sophia". Mitt and Dink were both ministers.

Left to Right   3. George Carter   6. Sara Walden   9. Mitt Walden, Rev.
1. Wanda Kitts   4. Dave Brandenburg, Rev. 7. Lassie Brandenburg 10. Dink Reynolds, Rev.
2. Edith James   5. Sophia Reynolds   8. Jess Bolton   11. Joe Moses, Rev.
        Around July, 1944 at Lick Creek at the White Bridge

A term frequently used down south is "Bless His Heart" or "Bless His Little Heart". This term, when used, has different meanings, and can be interpreted in different ways. If you are expressing sympathy or appreciation for something that someone might have done, you might say "Bless His Heart", but on the other hand if someone is doing something wrong, or something you don't approve of, you might say "Bless His Little Heart" in a derogatory tone. It all has to do with the look on your face and the inflection in your voice. Another thing that southern people do a lot is call each other "Honey". Men call women honey, women call men honey, hell my mom called everyone honey and I do the same. Amongst decent people it has no sexual connotations. Of course, amongst today's PC, Woke, anal, cancel culture crowd, it's sexual harassment.

I recently read "J. D. Vance's" book "Hillbilly Elegy" and He mentioned several times about his grandma and Grandpa using the "F" word frequently and all I can say is, I never heard my Granny or to the best of my memory, any other elderly southern person use that word. I'm not saying they didn't curse from time to time, but the "F" word wasn't high on their list of frequently used curse words. He must have emanated from a different strain of "Hillbilly's" than I did.

Some additional history about my uncle "Big John Long":

I mentioned earlier that my mom's older brother "John" was the only one of her immediate family that pretty much stayed in Campbell County Tennessee all his life. John was a unique character, fun to be around and was the basis for some funny stories. He could do about anything, but to the best of my knowledge, He usually worked in or around the coal mines.

John was a big man, not exceptionally tall, maybe 6 ft. 2 inches, but hard as a rock. I remember stopping by to visit him one evening and he was sitting in a galvanized tub in the middle of the kitchen floor, taking a bath, and he evidently had been working underground in the mines that day, because he was so black, all you could see was his teeth and eyeballs.

There is a hauntingly beautiful song, sang by Patty Loveless called "You'll never leave Harlan alive". It really makes you think about how dangerous and hard coal mining can be. Many men "did not leave Harlan alive".

I had quite a bit of exposure to "John" after I got out of the Marines and was staying with my Granny. John never had a car so he would get me to take him up on "stinking creek" on Friday evenings to get a gallon of moonshine (10 dollars a gallon). Now if you don't know where "stinking creek" is, I will tell you. When you are going south on I-75 and enter Tennessee, you start up over "Jellico Mountain" and it's not long until you will see an exit called "stinking creek" (Exit 144), that's it. I don't know if anyone's still making "shine", but I wouldn't be surprised.

One thing "John" liked to do was what he called "laying out" on Norris Lake overnight and fishing. His ideal of being well provisioned was some coffee, a block of cheese, some crackers, bologna, an onion, some "shine" and maybe an old blanket to lay down on. Sometimes if a boat was available, He would string a "Trot Line". If you don't know what a "trot line" is, it is basically a long fishing line, with equally spaced "baited hooks" hanging down below it. You stretch it across a body of water (using a boat) and then weight it down several feet below the water's surface. You then go back sometime later and do what they call "run the trot line" to remove the fish you might have caught. In the "Hank Williams Jr" song "Country Boy's Will Survive" he says, and I quote, "He could skin a buck and run a trot line", this is what he was talking about.

Other stories that come to mind about "John" are the one about a copperhead striking at him one time and hanging up in his pants leg. He just calmly leaned over and shot it off with his gun. Another instance, that I saw in person. He was keeping a rattlesnake in a box under his bed. I spent the night at his house one time, when he had that damn snake, and I didn't sleep a wink. As the story goes, he and one of his buddy's eventually got drunk and gave the snake to a church where they "handled snakes" and it bit the minister and killed him. If you think this is fiction, Google "snake handling churches".

Another time "John" wanted me to take him and a friend down near "Pall Mall", Tennessee on a weekend squirrel hunt. This is the area where the famous soldier from World War one "Alvin C. York" was born and raised. I think John had sort of a spiritual connection to "Sgt. York" because he asked me to take him down there more than once and John was an excellent shot, just like Sgt. York. The guy who went with us was named "Joe" and he had a reputation of being excellent with a knife. If you needed a horse gelded or a hog castrated, you called "Joe". The story going around was that Joe, a married couple and one other fellow were in the woods one time (drunk on moonshine) and they castrated this lady's husband. Since John and Joe were drinking "shine" that night, I slept with one eye open.

John also liked to shoot off dynamite on New Year's Eve and the fourth of July. He would take half sticks of dynamite, crimp the cap to the fuse with his teeth and then stick it into the half stick of dynamite. He would do that to about 6 sticks and then line them up on the end of cross ties (on the railroad spur that went past his house) and light the fuses. Boom, Boom, baby!

A little more about southern folks and southern/country music:

I don't believe you can write a book with an appreciable amount of southern content without talking about southern music. It stretches all the way from traditional country, to bluegrass, to the blues, to rock 'n' roll, not to mention gospel, jazz, rap, and soul. Over the years, southern music has grown and changed, but the southern states have always been a major source for America's authentic sound. There's not many towns or hollows where there's not some country folks who can sing beautifully, pick a banjo, strum a guitar, play a fiddle or some other traditional southern instrument, and many are self-taught.

I personally prefer, what I would call Pop, Country classics and Gospel. Some of my favorites are listed below, and there's many more:

George Jones "He stopped loving her today", "Who's gonna fill their shoes".

Gene Watson's "Farewell party".

Patsy Cline's "Crazy", "Walkin after midnight", "I fall to pieces".

Vince Gills "Go rest high on that mountain", "When I call your name".

The Cathedrals (George Younce) "Suppertime", "Thanks to Calvary".

Iris Dement "Leaning on The Everlasting Arms".

The Isaacs "Mama's Teaching Angels How to Sing", "Sweet Holy Spirit".

Ray Price's "For the good time's" (written by Kris Kristofferson).

Elvis "Dixie, An American trilogy", "Peace in the valley", "Amazing grace", "Hurt", "My way", etc.

Johnny Cash "Folsom prison blues", "A boy named Sue", and many more.

Kris Kristofferson "Why me lord", "Sunday morning coming down", "Me and Bobby McGee".

Dolly Parton's "I will always love you", "Islands in the stream" with Kenny Rogers.

The Band "The Weight" and "The night they drove old Dixie down".

John Schneider "I've been around enough to know" and "country girls".

Loretta Lynn: "Coal Miner's Daughter".

David Allen Coe's "You never even called me by my name."

Eva Cassidy "Danny boy", "Somewhere over the rainbow".

Bobbie Bare "Green, green grass of home", "Detroit city" and "Streets of Baltimore".

Justin Timberlake and Chris Stapleton "Tennessee Whiskey".

The Osborne Brothers "Rocky Top".

Alabama "old Flame".

 Another thing that is so traditional about the south, many of the country artists say they got started singing in church and southern folks love gospel music.

A couple of other things that were important to southern men was their Rifle or Shotgun, their Pocket knife, their smoking tobacco and chewing tobacco. If they didn't have anything else to do, they liked to compare knifes, sit around, and whittle and spit a lot. "Case" and "Buck" Knifes are brands that were and are still popular.

I guess to summarize all this, I would say, "Southern People" are for the most part, hardworking, honest, patriotic, independent, God-fearing people who don't particularly trust outsiders, and are hesitant to take strangers into their inner circle (until they get to know them). They also like pickup trucks, Jeeps, atv's, hunting, fishing, a good hunting dog, football, country music and good southern cooking.

Bless your hearts Y'all and God bless the South "yesterday, today, and forever".

EPILOGUE:

Finally, I want to leave you with this: My dear wife "Roberta" passed away almost four years ago (2018). I love her and miss her so much. It just tore my heart out. We were married for over sixty-one years. It may sound strange, but I take flowers to the cemetery about once a month and talk to her, tell her how our family is doing, our Grandchildren (10) and now our great Grandchildren (7).

What I would like to say to each of you personally is this: It is tragic when you lose someone you love and it's especially sad, when you can't even hug them and tell them you love them, say goodbye, and have a proper funeral, which has been the case for so many people during this Covid-19 pandemic. I'm very sorry for you all.

One other thing I might mention. "Elvis" and I were born in the same month, same year (January 1935) and the last song to be played at my funeral when I pass on will be "Elvis" singing the "American Trilogy", which includes "Dixie".

The last song played at the Veterans cemetery when I am buried will be "Taps", played by a Marine Corp's honor guard. "Once a Marine, always a Marine".

Cpl. Richard J. Davis Jr.

Me and my dear wife "Roberta". She passed away on Nov. 4th, 2018.

I know exactly where you are honey, and I will see you before too long.

Chapter 12: Family Legacy Photo's.

The Walden's and Reynold's:

Theodore Walden and Sarah Eller (Reynolds) Walden.

Roberta Leigh (Walden) Davis   Geraldine Ann (Walden) Lawson

Two beautiful young Southern ladies.

Papaw Walden's restored 1969, Chevy C20 truck.

John Frank Walden, Mary Jane (Reynolds) Walden and Lonnie (Dink) Reynolds.

The Walden Boys: L to R, Mitt, Oscar, Earnest, William, Theodore at their father (John Franks) funeral c.1962. The five Boys were all born and raised in "Walden Hollow".

The Reynolds Family: Minton, Oscar, Lonnie (Dink), Earnest, Mary and Sarah. They were all born and raised on "Hickory Creek".

Ben Reynolds Photo

Unavailable

Julia Ann (Jordan) Reynolds, Wife of Benjamin Reynolds

John Frank Walden and wife Luerany Bolton. He kind of reminds me of "Doc. Holiday" in the movie "Tombstone" with that big mustache. John Frank was a very independent person and from what I've been told, the older he got, the more independent he got and the bigger his mustache got.

1 Eli
2 Mary Elizabeth
3 Jackson
4 John Frank
5 Matilda
6 Will
7 Sol Sloman

This is "John Frank Walden" and his siblings. Shown are his brothers and sisters. L to R: Eli, Jackson, Mary Elizabeth, John Frank, Matilda, Will and Sol.

The Long's: (The only photos I have of the "Davis" family ancestors appear earlier in book, My Dads' father, mother, and sister).

L to R: Anna Clyde Fraker, Amanda Emalyn (Long) Olsen, William Howard (Bill) Long, Me and My Mom (Mattie Mildred (Long) Davis at Norris Lake (probably about 1945).

My Moms Brothers and Sisters (one photo is missing, Sister Willie Mae).

William Howard (Bill) Long

John Franklin Long

Amanda Emalyn (Long) Olsen

LOTTIE ELLA LONG WAGONER
AGE 21

Lottie Ella (Long) Wagoner

1954
RHODA L. NORMAN, AGE 50
(1954)

Rhoda Annie (Long) Norman

Ruth Jeanette (Long) Fraker

Mattie Mildred (Long) Davis (My Mom)

Rhoda Annie Long, William Burke Franklin Long (Grandpa), Willie Mae Long, Annie Sophia (Wicks) Long (Grandma), Lottie Ella Long.

Nancy Adeline (Burke) Long
Grandpa Long's Mother

Sophia Ann (Murphy) Wicks
Grandma Long's Mother

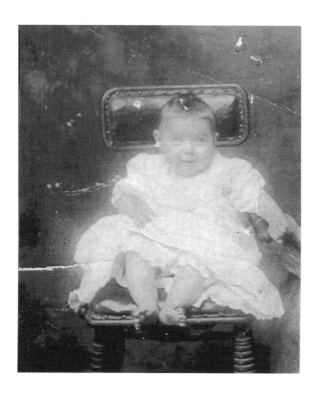

This was a "Tintype" of My Mom, "Mattie Mildred Long" c.1913

Chapter 13: Some additional "Long" family history.

Although I wrote about several members of the "Long" family earlier in the book, I also wanted to include several interesting stories that came to light in a biography about the "Long" family put together on "Ancestry.com" by one of my cousins.

Moses Long and Nancy Elizabeth Burke were Grandpa Long's parents and Theodore Wick's, and Sophia Anne (Koon) Murphy were Grandma Long's parents. This is pertinent because Granny Long's mother was ¼ Shawnee Indian. The Long's (Lang's) were German, and the Burke's were Irish (See note below). Moses Long served in the Confederate States Army during the civil war. He was in the battle of Vicksburg (was captured by the Union Army and later paroled) and then returned to the Confederate Army and fought in the battles of Missionary Ridge and Lookout Mountain.

William Preston Burk was Nancy Elizabeth Burke's father. The war brought tragedy to the Burke family. As the war drew close to Walker County, Georgia, William started hiding horses for local families on Lookout Mountain to keep them from being taken by Union soldiers. Eventually he was captured and taken prisoner. Word later came back to the family that William died enroute to a Union prison.

George Long was born in Bedford County, Va. and during his boyhood years his family moved to Sevier County, Tennessee. George eventually became a minister of the gospel (Primitive Baptist Faith) and served as a Pastor at "The Providence Baptist Church" in Sevier County for about twenty Years. George and most of his family moved to McMinn County, Tennessee in about 1827. In McMinn County, George continued his preaching and mission work. During January 1849, while delivering a sermon he became sick, while returning home on horseback. He became so ill that he was compelled to dismount and lie down by the side of the road. He was found there by friends, and with loving care, they attempted to take him home. But, before they reached his home, he passed away. Reverend Georges last words were "Ring the Old Gospel Bell".

Johannes Long was born in Manheim, Lancaster County, pa. in 1749 (He Died in1817). He was a revolutionary war soldier and served in the "First Virginia Regiment", "Eighth Continental Line" in General Peter Muhlengreg's Brigade during the American Revolution. He served at Brandywine Creek, Germantown, Valley Forge and Princeton. He was also with General Washington's forces at the crossing of the Delaware. The dates work because George Washington crossed the Delaware on December 25th and 26th, 1776.

Portrayal of George Washington crossing the Delaware

The Long Family: (in Chronological order).

William Burke Franklin Long, Annie Sophia Wicks, Roxanna E. Williams (Grandpa Long and his two wife's).

Theodore Wicks, Sophia Ann (Koon) Murphy (Grandma Long's parents).

Moses Long, Nancy Elizabeth Burke (Grandpa Long's parents).

John Albert Long, Jane Allen (Moses Long's parents).

William Preston Burke (Nancy Elizabeth Burke's father).

George Long, Elizabeth (Nancy?) Maples (John Albert Long's parents).

Johannes Long, Mary Haynes (George Long's parents).

Johannes Nicholas Lang, Anna Schnebele (Johannes Long's parents).

Johannes Lang, Anna Elizabeth Korlen (Johannes Nicholas Lang's parents).

Johannes Lang, Dorothea Schimmer (Johannes Lang's parents).

Note: "Lang" was the alternate spelling for "Long" at one time. Also "Burk" was spelled two different ways on Ancestry.com. Some places it's "Burk" and other places it's "Burke".

Chapter 14: Some Family Vacation Suggestions.

First, I want to say unequivocally that me, my wife, and family did not go on a lot of vacations. We could not afford it, but we did go to several places that left us with some everlasting memories.

I just got to thinking, since we are hopefully coming out of this Covid-19 lockdown of the last two years, a lot of people might be debating, where is a nice place for a family vacation or to take a little day trip?

Places you might like:

1. Canaan Valley, Blackwater Falls, West Virginia: Beautiful area with lots of outdoor activities (including Skiing). Spruce Knob is nearby with an elevation of 4,863 feet. There is a viewing tower on top. It is so cold, and the wind blows so hard up there in the wintertime that some of the trees only have limbs and leaves on one side.
2. Frankenmuth, Michigan: Bronner's Christmas Wonderland, two great chicken restaurants, beautiful flowers, Bavarian culture, Bavarian restaurants, breweries, wineries, shopping, and lots of outdoor activities.
3. Mackinac Island, Michigan: Accessed by ferry from Mackinaw city, or St. Ignace, no cars allowed, you get around by walking, bicycle or horse drawn carriage, very historic, beautiful scenery, the grand hotel, golf, forts, shopping, candy makers, restaurants, etc. For you film lovers, there was a movie filmed mostly on Mackinac Island at the Grand Hotel in 1980 called "Somewhere in Time". It starred Jane Seymour and Christopher Reeve.
4. Gatlinburg, Pigeon Forge and the Smokies: Too many activities to list, but I always enjoyed eating at the "Apple Barn" and the "Old Mill" restaurants, going to Cade's cove, hiking, camping, wild animals, etc. This can be a day trip for a lot of family's east of the Mississippi river.
5. Puerto Rico: I lived there for 4-1/2 years as a teenager (see Chapter 4, page 25 for some of the places we used to go).
6. Cruises: We took the typical Caribbean cruise: "Cozumel, Cayman Islands, Jamaica" and then later flew to "Hawaii" and cruised the four main islands for a week. I think the two things that impressed me the most were the night when the ship stopped and turned out the lights and we saw the "Lava" from the "Kilauea Volcano" flowing into the ocean (it's been erupting since 1983).

That lava hardens and the island gets a little bigger. The other thing was going to the "Arizona Memorial". It takes your breath away. 1,177 brave service members were killed when the Japanese sank the "USS Arizona" on Dec 7th, 1941. It is the final resting place of 1,102 of the brave Sailors and Marines who died that day. Approx. thirty or so survivors have asked to be cremated thru the years and divers have placed their remains in the sunken ship in a secure location. The "Arizona Memorial" straddles the sunken ship and although it was sunk over 80 years ago, about nine gallons of oil is still coming to the ocean surface each day.

7. If you are traveling on I-75 thru Tennessee, another thing you might enjoy seeing are the "Elk" from the "Hatfield Knob Viewing Tower" in the "North Cumberland Wildlife Management Area". The main entry point to this area is about seven miles north of LaFollette, Tennessee on US25W (the "red gate" on top of Peabody Mountain). You can also get to "Hatfield Knob" from the "Ride Royal Blue ATV resort and campground" on "Stinking Creek Road" (which runs between I-75 and 25W, Exit 144). There is also a live streaming camera of the "ELK" on the internet from the "Hatfield Knob" viewing tower.

Elk at "Hatfield Knob" in Campbell County, Tennessee. See paragraph 7 above.

8. Chattanooga: There is a lot to see and do around Chattanooga, Lookout Mountain (lots of Civil War history), Ruby Falls, Rock city, The Incline Railway, The Tennessee Aquarium, "Chattanooga Choo Choo" to name a few. There is also a lot of outdoor activities.

9. We took a nice driving trip one time where we went north from Cincinnati, east on the Pennsylvania turnpike, south to Washington, DC, east to Ocean city, Maryland, south on the peninsula on the east side of the Chesapeake Bay (Assateague, Island) and then across the 17-mile-long bridge/tunnel into Norfolk, Virginia. We then came back north to Cincinnati.

Chapter 15: My opinion of Presidents, Parties and Policies.

I guess I should state that I am basically a conservative and normally embrace conservative policies and ideas, but I am not so rigid that I would not support a liberal ideal if it's in the best interest of all the American people. I also think that many of our politicians (both Democrats and Republicans) are in politics for the money, the adulation, the prestige, and for the influence they have, that allows them to bring "home the bacon", so to speak, for their wealthy constituents, their donors, and themselves. They all seem to have a lot more money when they leave office than when they went in. I wonder why?

Although I voted for President Trump, I will be the first to admit that He has his flaws, as a person and as a politician. He is sometimes crude, egotistical, exaggerates a lot and always wants to be the center of attention, but He did have some significant accomplishments while President. Some examples are as follows: The tax cut, penal reform, reduction of many duplicative federal regulations, a vastly improved economy (before covid-19), energy independence, improved trade policies, increased funding for the military, the keystone XL pipeline and the border wall were being built, he pulled us out of the Iran nuclear deal, the Paris accord (which was biased against the United States), cut funding to the W.H.O. (which is China's lap dog), had a "repartee" with North Korea's leader and was making progress towards peace in the middle east.

We do not currently have a comprehensive immigration policy, but there were agreements in place under President Trump to help stem the flow of illegals, unlike what's happening right now. The current situation at the border is totally out of control. The human trafficking, the flow of drugs, guns, gang members, probable terrorists, illegals, etc. entering this country right now is at historic levels (estimated to be at least two million since Joe Biden took office. No one knows the real number because of all "the so called got aways").

Now what has President Biden proposed so far. He stopped construction on the Keystone XL pipeline, shut down oil exploration/drilling in ANWR, etc., stopped construction on the border wall (which was already funded). Many people may not know it, but there is 100 million dollars' worth of material for the wall sitting down there in the weather rusting and ruining, stopped issuing new permits for drilling on federal land, gas prices are soaring, baby formula is in short supply, inflation is the highest it's been in forty years. He also restored funding to the W.H.O. and rejoined the Paris climate accord.

Bernie Sanders (an avowed socialist) wants to increase federal spending by six trillion dollars and institute all these socialist programs. If passed, this would be a major power grab by the Democratic party and a huge step towards Communism/ Marxism. The motive behind this is to make everyone equal and co-dependent on the federal government and once that happens, the government can tell you what to do, what to say, where you can travel, etc. Nikita Khrushchev, former communist leader, said in 1956 and I quote "We will take America without firing a shot. We do not have to invade the U.S. We will destroy you from within".

This "Critical race Theory" that the liberals and our so called "Woke" society is wanting to teach in our schools is totally wrong and will have a lasting effect on our children. Racism, in any form is completely wrong, but raising a generation of children who are ashamed of being white, have a guilt complex and low self-esteem is not the answer. Also, in my opinion, teaching young children from kindergarten thru the 3rd grade about sexual orientation and gender identity is not only confusing to them, but is wrong and should be forbidden.

I am also thoroughly disgusted by the lies and omissions being espoused by the Democratic party and the liberal media. They are constantly talking about white Officers killing black people and discriminating against them, but rarely do they talk about blacks killing blacks and black on black crime, in mostly Democratically controlled cities. When so called "Protestors" are breaking windows, looting, destroying property, Hi-jacking cars, assaulting police officers, etc., the media usually calls it peaceful protests. Bullshit, they are criminals, and in many cases, they are destroying businesses that people have worked all their lives to establish and it's their only means of livelihood. Many businesses are owned by minorities and immigrants.

I have never seen, by many, such a level of hostility, mistrust, disrespect toward their fellow citizens. Liberals versus conservatives, Democrats versus Republicans, Blacks versus Whites. Compromise seems to be a thing of the past. Since everyone has a camera and recording devices in their hands, no matter what you say or do (even if there's nothing wrong with it) it will be misinterpreted, and immediately disseminated over social media and many are then accused, tried, and convicted in the eyes of the bigots, who could care less about what really happened. This is true of many politicians, television personalities and the print media. If it isn't reigned in soon, "anarchy" will follow and it's already happening in some of our major Democratically controlled cities.

I also think a dangerous precedent is being set by destroying and defacing Civil War statues and monuments and at the same time disregarding southern history. I agree that slavery and segregation were abhorrent, terribly demeaning to African Americans and should have never happened, but there are literally thousands of monuments, plaques, buildings, Army bases, cemeteries, etc. around the country named after Southern generals. Defacing them and tearing them down is not only going to be extremely expensive and disruptive, but a bone of contention between blacks and whites, liberals, and conservatives for years to come. Is that the kind of dissension and hatred that we really need?

I am a staunch supporter of the second amendment and think all law-abiding citizens have the right to keep and bear arms to protect themselves and their families. One thing you should all remember, "people kill people, guns by themselves don't kill people". There are some potential changes to the law that might help deter gun violence and I have conveyed them to the President, more than once. See my letter to President Trump in chapter 16.

Politically correct, Woke, Cancel Culture Bullshit, talk of Sexual Misconduct, Racism, etc. That's about all we hear these days on certain tv networks. My personal philosophy is simply this. "Be friendly, Treat everyone with respect and expect the same in return. Don't let race or gender be a determining factor". It is not wrong to tell a lady her hair looks nice, or her outfit is pretty. It is the touching or vulgar suggestive remarks that are wrong. A little flirting amongst singles is fine. How are people supposed to meet, marry, pro-create, etc. Duh? If I was a young man in today's uptight society, I would be a nervous wreck. Also, frequently, the most qualified applicant can't get a job because of his or her political persuasion. If they do get the job, others set out to destroy them. All you must do is accuse someone of "sexual misconduct" or "Racism" (weather it's true or false) and a person's life or career can be ruined. What has happened to us as a country, as a people? We are not only trying to deal with this terrible pandemic, but the "joy of living" is being taken away from us by these hypocritical politicians, activists, and media types. The lies and hateful vitriol being spewed is dangerous and disgusting.

I am opposed to "Reparations" and the government paying off "student debt". It is not fair to the people who have worked for years to pay off their loans. I also know that the tuition charged at many of our universities (particularly Ivy league schools) is extremely high and since they have billions of dollars in Endowments (i.e., Harvard 53.2 billion, Yale 42.3 billion, Princeton, 37.7 billion, Penn 20.5, Stanford, 37.8 billion, etc.) Why don't they refund some of that money to the students? Also, why don't they reduce their tuition?

As for "Reparations", why should hard working people today (of all races) pay for something wrong, that our forefathers did over one hundred fifty years ago? Are we going to pay "Reparations" to all the young men (or their family's) who were seriously injured or killed fighting in numerous wars through the years to try and protect our country and our freedoms?

I am also opposed to "abortion" except in the case of rape, incest or to protect the health of the mother. The estimate is that there have been over 63 million legal abortions in the United States in the last 49 years. Where would these pro-abortion activists be if their mothers had decided to abort them years ago? Who gives anyone the right, to determine who lives and who dies? In my opinion, poor innocent babies don't deserve that fate. That's not what the Good Lord intended.

My Uncle Bill Long holding me in 1935. I wouldn't be here if my Mother would have decided to abort me?

Chapter 16: Letters from Me to President Trump and His Responses.

Richard Davis

Feb. 26, 2018

President Donald J Trump
1600 Pennsylvania Ave.
Washington, D.C. 20500

Dear Mr. President,

The following is a compilation of some ideas and suggestions that I have regarding potential gun control legislation and school safety.

Gun control:

1. Raising the age to purchase semi-automatic rifles (ie, the AR-15) is probably a waste of time and energy for two reasons. A-the NRA won't agree, and B-there are hundreds of millions of guns out there, and if a person wants to buy a semi-automatic weapon, they don't have to go to a gun store.

2. Elimination of bump stocks.

3. Better and more comprehensive back ground checks.

4. More stringent gun show oversight (a lot of deals take place in the parking lot, etc).

5. Stricter control of on-line sales. (Guns are supposed to be shipped to a licensed dealer for transaction to be completed and guns to be registered, but how in the hell do you enforce that, when all the buyer and seller have to do is agree to meet some other place).

6. Magazine capacity should be looked at. (although this probably won't fly with the NRA).

7. The "mental health" issue is extremely important and has many facets to it and should be looked at by "mental health professionals" and they should make legislative suggestions.

8. Don't expect to solve this too fast because there are federal, state and local laws to consider. Maybe changes would help, but in reality there is no total solution.

School safety:

1. There should be very limited access to schools for non- students.

2. Electronic locks on all access doors and bullet proof glass.

3. Secure, lockable doors on all class rooms.

3. Armed plain clothed security people in all schools.

4. All students and teachers should have photo I.D.

5. There are small bio-metric safes available (that handguns can be stored in) that only certified security people would be allowed to open.

Respectfully,

Richard J. Davis Jr.

Richard J. Davis

President Donald J. Trump   May 4, 2020
1600 Pennsylvania Ave.
Washington, D.C.

Dear Mr. President,

   I am part of your base and plan on voting for you in November, but I would respectfully
like to offer you some advice. I am an ex-marine who served in Korea and have seen and heard
pretty much everything, but you see Mr. President, there's this kinder and gentler faction that
have not, and you need some of their votes in November, particularly women and indepen-
dents. I understand your combative style and ego, (we old marines also have big egos, it's in
our DNA). I don't know how you could be much different being raised up in the rough and
tumble world of New York real estate, dealing with unions, politicians, etc.

   Now here is my advice. One: accentuate your accomplishments (foreign and domestic), two:
it's ok to berate the Media (fake news), but don't call them bad names (that sells well with
your base, but not with the kinder and gentler types), three: give the environmentalists some
things they can relate to, four: don't fire everyone who disagrees with you, some of them are
smart people, five: be tough, but don't be afraid to show a little humility from time to time
(that plays well with the women), six: review your Speeches in advance and don't adlib so
much (that can sometimes get you in trouble), seven: try and be very accurate with all your
statements (you have a lot of enemies out there and they never quit looking for something to
criticize you for), and last but not least: challenge your speech writers to come up with some
"memorable lines" as we head toward the election. There have been many things said by
presidents thru the years that really stick with people.

God bless you and your family and get some rest. Semper fi,
Richard J Davis Jr.

PS: I lost my wife in 2018. We had been married over 61 years. It tore my heart out. My point
being this: all these people are dying during this pandemic (Moms, Dads, Grandparents,
Brothers, Sisters, Children, etc.) and their loved ones don't even get to hug their necks and tell
them they love them. A lot of them are not even able to have proper funerals (so tragic).

Mr. President, tell them you love them and God bless them. That will mean so much.

Richard J. Davis

President Donald J. Trump   JULY 15, 2020
1600 Pennsylvania Ave.
Washington, D.C.

Dear Mr. President,
   I wrote you two letters previously outlining my views on what I thought you should focus on
to get re-elected. Everything has changed in the last several months and my views have
changed dramatically. These are my latest assessments, which I hope you will consider.

1. Focus strongly on law and order, safety, security, etc. Don't cave or pander in any way to
these damn Anarchists or Democrats.They are looking for signs of weakness.

2. I believe there will be massive attempts at voter fraud in November. It is also my belief that
BLM, Antifa, etc. will try to scare and intimidate people at the polling places. A lot of older
people will not get out and vote. One lone security person (after what's going on now) is not
going to be reassuring at all. Mail- in ballots can also be compromised.

3. You need to stress repeatedly how Democratic Governors, Mayors, etc. have allowed all of
this lawlessness that's going on. This destruction of property, looting, defacing and destruction
of monuments, statues, etc., has got to stop. It's disgusting, shameful and disrespectful.

4. Mr. President, a lot of weak kneed people will vote for "Biden" because they believe that
everything will calm down if he's elected. In my opinion, that is not what's going to happen.
What's going to happen is this: He will be pushed aside very quickly, the "VP" will take over
and Socialists/Anarchists will be running the country. If they win the house and senate, they
will start pushing for "reparations", tax increases, etc. and other things immediately.

5. Show some humility (that plays well with the women). You will need some women and
Independent votes. A good last line to a speech is "I love our country, I am so sorry for all the
families who have lost loved ones to this terrible pandemic and in many cases didn't even get
to say goodbye. So sad, God bless you all". Another good last line is "My fellow Americans, if
you don't vote Republican in November, I believe you will regret it for the rest of your lives.

6. Accentuate your accomplishments, the economy, etc., but that is not what people are
transfixed on right now. Get your people on the same page, there is too much chaos.

Respectfully submitted,
Richard J. Davis Jr.   (I am a former Marine, 1953-1956, Korea,   )

THE WHITE HOUSE
WASHINGTON

August 14, 2018

Mr. Richard Davis
Walton, Kentucky

Dear Mr. Davis,

Thank you for taking the time to share your views regarding school and community safety.

No one should ever feel unsafe in our Nation's schools. Following the senseless acts of violence that have occurred, I have brought together students, parents, educators, and legislators to discuss ways to improve safety in our schools and communities. My Administration will continue to enforce Federal law and work with State and local officials to secure our schools, keep firearms out of the wrong hands, and protect Americans from violent criminals.

Additionally, my Administration is tackling the difficult issue of mental health. We must ensure that those individuals living with mental illness have access to evidence-based treatment and services, and we must fight the stigma associated with mental illness, which often prevents those who are suffering from seeking care. For this reason, my fiscal year 2019 budget request to Congress includes new funding to improve access to evidence-based treatment for the seriously mentally ill.

When a horrendous act of violence occurs, it shocks the conscience of our Nation and fills our hearts with immense grief. We will unite together to create a culture in our country that embraces the dignity of life and creates deep and meaningful connections with our classmates, colleagues, and neighbors.

Thank you again for writing. One of my highest priorities as President is the safety of the American people, especially our Nation's young people.

Sincerely,

Print

Date: Thursday, March 1, 2018 9:30 AM
From: The White House <noreply@whitehouse.gov>
To:
Subject: Thank You For Your Message

THE WHITE HOUSE

WASHINGTON
March 1, 2018

I appreciate you taking the time to send your thoughts and suggestions. My staff will share your email with me shortly, and I look forward to responding to it soon.

In 2016, nearly 175 Americans died from a drug overdose each day. Too many of our fellow Americans have been lost due to the scourge of drug abuse. It is plaguing families and communities across our Nation, robbing so many of their potential.

My Administration is fighting the opioid crisis on all fronts. Today we are hosting a summit at the White House to face this challenge as a national family, with both conviction and unity.

Join us live, or learn more about my Administrations strategy to combat addiction in America.

Thank you again for taking the time to write.

With best wishes,

If you wish to receive regular email updates from the White House, please Click Here. You may also follow President Trump and the White House on Facebook, Instagram, Twitter, and YouTube.

White House Website | Privacy Policy | Contact the White House

Print

Date: Thursday, February 22, 2018 12:40 PM

From: The White House <noreply@whitehouse.gov>

To:

Subject: Thank You For Your Message

THE WHITE HOUSE

WASHINGTON
February 22, 2018

I appreciate you taking the time to share your thoughts and suggestions. My staff will share your email with me shortly, and I look forward to reading it.

I was truly touched by the students, parents, and educators who joined me for a listening session at the White House yesterday. Each of the participants demonstrated incredible courage by sharing their heartbreaking personal stories.

To continue this important discussion, today I will welcome both State and local officials to the White House for a dialogue about the actions we must take to protect our childrenactions that actually make a difference.

My Administration is already taking significant measures to ensure the safety of Americans, especially our Nations children, and we will not rest until our schools are free from violence and fear.

With best wishes,

If you wish to receive regular email updates from the White House, please Click Here. You may also follow President Trump and the White House on Facebook, Instagram, Twitter, and YouTube.

White House Website | Privacy Policy | Contact the White House

Print

Date: Wednesday, January 24, 2018 7:02 PM
From: The White House <noreply@whitehouse.gov>
To:
Subject: Response to Your Message

THE WHITE HOUSE
WASHINGTON

Dear Richard:

Thank you for taking the time to express your views on recognizing Jerusalem as the capital of Israel and moving the United States Embassy to Israel from Tel Aviv to Jerusalem.

On December 6, 2017, I signed a proclamation recognizing Jerusalem, the ancient capital of the Jewish people, as the capital of Israel. This recognition enjoys broad, bipartisan support in Congress. In fact, in 2017, the United States Senate unanimously reaffirmed the Jerusalem Embassy Act of 1995, which urged recognition of Jerusalem as the capital of Israel.

Additionally, I have instructed the Department of State to relocate the United States Embassy to Israel from Tel Aviv to Jerusalem. The safety and security of Americans and our assets in the region will be our top priority at every step in this process.

I recognize that the status of Jerusalem is a highly sensitive issue, and the United States remains committed to achieving a lasting peace agreement between the Israelis and the Palestinians. Recognizing Jerusalem as Israels capital and announcing the relocation of our embassy do not reflect a departure from the strong commitment of the United States to facilitating a lasting peace agreement. The United States continues to take no position on any final status issues. The specific boundaries of Israeli sovereignty in Jerusalem are subject to final status negotiations between the parties. The United States is not taking a position on boundaries or borders and will support a two-state solution if agreed to by both sides.

Thank you again for writing. To learn more about my decision to recognize Jerusalem as the capital of Israel, please visit WhiteHouse.gov/JerusalemEmbassy. As President, my greatest hope above all is for peace, which is never beyond the grasp of those who are willing to reach for it.

Sincerely,

WWW.WHITEHOUSE.GOV

Print

Date: Wednesday, March 28, 2018 6:56 PM
From: The White House <noreply@whitehouse.gov>
To:
Subject: Response to Your Message

THE WHITE HOUSE
WASHINGTON

Dear Richard:

Thank you for taking the time to express your views regarding our Second Amendment rights.

My Administration is committed to upholding the Second Amendment and defending the right of our free and sovereign people to keep and bear arms. Our Founders fully understood that the ability of law-abiding citizens to defend themselves, their families, and their property from harm is a hallmark of a free people.

Over the eight years before I took office, the Second Amendment was under continuous attack from policies that made it difficult or impossible for law-abiding citizens to purchase firearms. I have already begun to reverse this dangerous trend, and I continue to work to ensure that your Government is abiding by the Second Amendment and does not infringe on your rights.

We took first steps to restore the Second Amendment in February of 2017 when I signed legislation nullifying an Internal Revenue Service (IRS) rule that would have allowed the IRS to conduct mental health investigations of Social Security recipients and turn their names over to the National Instant Criminal Background Check System.

In addition to administrative steps, I look forward to working with Congress to pass laws that will protect the Second Amendment from Federal overreach in the future. These laws will hopefully serve to further protect this key constitutional right.

Thank you again for writing. As President, I am steadfastly committed to protecting your rights and the security of our Nation.

Sincerely,

Made in the USA
Columbia, SC
15 February 2023

12421903R00059